BOOMERS

BOOMERS

The Men and Women
Who Promised Freedom and
Delivered Disaster

HELEN ANDREWS

SENTINEL

SENTINEL
An imprint of Penguin Random House LLC
penguinrandomhouse.com

Most Sentinel books are available at a discount when purchased in quantity for sales
promotions or corporate use. Special editions, which include personalized covers, excerpts,
and corporate imprints, can be created when purchased in large quantities. For more information,
please call (212) 572-2232 or email specialmarkets@penguinrandomhouse.com. Your local
bookstore can also assist with discounted bulk purchases using the Penguin Random
House corporate Business-to-Business program. For assistance in locating a
participating retailer, email B2B@penguinrandomhouse.com.

LIBRARY OF CONGRESS CATALOGING-IN-PUBLICATION DATA
Names: Andrews, Helen (Millennial journalist) author.
Title: Boomers : the men and women who promised freedom and delivered
disaster / Helen Andrews.
Description: New York : Sentinel, 2021. | Includes bibliographical references and index.
Identifiers: LCCN 2020036188 (print) | LCCN 2020036189 (ebook) |
ISBN 9780593086759 (hardcover) | ISBN 9780593086766 (ebook)
Subjects: LCSH: Baby boom generation—United States—History. | Baby boom
generation—United States—Biography. | United
States—History—Biography. | Liberty. | Generation Y—United
States—Social conditions—21st century.
Classification: LCC HN59.2 .A537 2021 (print) | LCC HN59.2 (ebook) |
DDC 305.20973—dc23
LC record available at https://lccn.loc.gov/2020036188
LC ebook record available at https://lccn.loc.gov/2020036189

Printed in the United States of America
1   3   5   7   9   10   8   6   4   2

BOOK DESIGN BY LUCIA BERNARD

For John R. Rittelmeyer (1955-2019)

Contents

Preface

———

When my editor at *First Things* magazine suggested that I write a book about the baby boomers modeled on Lytton Strachey's *Eminent Victorians*, my estimate of his literary judgment, which I already rated highly because he printed my stuff, increased further. *Eminent Victorians* is a great book and, what is far more rare, a successful book. It hit what it aimed at. The Victorians had less influence on the world when Strachey was done with them. To do the same for the boomers was so obviously a good idea that I forgave my editor for elaborating on my suitability for the project by saying, "You're like Strachey; you're an essayist, and you're mean."

Eminent Victorians, for those who don't know it, was a collection of short biographical portraits published in May 1918, in the waning days of World War I, and never was a book more fortunate in its timing. It arrived in London shops just as Germany's spring offensive was faltering and American troops were finally arriving in numbers on the western front. As victory became close enough to contemplate and the psychological clench of wartime began to relax, the people of Britain started to ask themselves whether it had all been worth it.

Among those who concluded that it had not, there were many who saw the war as something worse than an error of judgment. Their suspicion, which Strachey's book put into words for them, was that the men who had brought Britain into the war and all the values those men had believed in must have been not just mistaken but fundamentally corrupt.

The four Victorians Strachey chose to attack had always been held in high esteem: Cardinal Manning, the Roman Catholic archbishop known for his social work; Thomas Arnold, the Rugby headmaster who invented the English public school as we know it; General Charles Gordon, the martyr of Khartoum; and Florence Nightingale, the one modern readers have heard of. To blame these national heroes for the Somme was a stretch, and in Nightingale's case positively perverse. Nevertheless, Strachey attacked his targets with an oedipal fury, perhaps because these four figures, though long dead, felt oppressively present to him as architects of the world he inhabited.

It was not *what* the Victorians believed that Strachey rebelled against so much as their believing in anything at all. Strachey himself was a pure aesthete. "Only two things I find amuse me," he once told Leonard Woolf, "wit and the flesh." This insouciance eventually worked against his credibility when it became clear he had no alternative set of values to offer, but for *Eminent Victorians* his ironic pose only helped. It gave the book a light touch. The Victorians could survive being proven wrong. They could not survive being made to look ridiculous.

The first edition sold out nine printings in two years. It did not matter that many of the things Strachey wrote were simply false, as he happily admitted. War-weary book buyers cared about only one thing: the people who had gotten the country into such a mess deserved a shellacking, and Strachey had given it to them. As Cyril Connolly once said, the nice thing about the 1920s was that "in those days, whenever you didn't get on with your father, you had all the glorious dead on your side."

And those of us who would attack the baby boomers, what do we have on our side?

I have no quarrel with my parents, who were both born in the 1950s. My father, who died while this manuscript was being written, was a liberal Southern lawyer of the Atticus Finch type and, like Atticus, beyond reproach. My mother was a bit of a hippie when she was younger—she majored in pottery at a college that no longer exists—but the only thing I have to reproach her for on that score is that I never learned how to put on makeup. They were wonderful parents, and I'm very grateful to them.

Whatever my editor at *First Things* might say, I don't feel this book was written in a spirit of meanness. As I was drafting a list of boomers to profile, I found that I had no interest at all in writing about buffoons and psychopaths, however colorful some of them were. Instead, I was drawn to the boomers who had all the elements of greatness but whose effect on the world was tragically and often ironically contrary to their intentions. Their destructiveness came from their virtues as much as their vices. I was going to spend months, even years with these people living in my head. I did not want to pick anyone for whom I felt contempt.

On the other hand, I do feel some of the moral indignation that animated Strachey's readers. I graduated from college in 2008 already with a sense that the millennials were, in some deep spiritual sense, a dispossessed generation. Then the financial crash came, and the sense of dispossession became more literal. Those were lean years for me and my friends, made worse by the burden of student debt, which boomers urged us to take on as much of as we could in order to go to the best school that would have us. The recession's headwind on our careers has put millennials years behind in achieving the standard material indicators of adulthood, like marriage and buying a house. But as long as millennials are trapped in the Tinder cycle or on the career track and putting off childbearing anyway, what would we need to buy a house for?

I began this book thinking that it could articulate the same anti-boomer brief that all my millennial friends seemed to be arriving at independently. Boomers were the people who scolded us for complaining about student loan debt when, in their day, you could work off a semester's tuition in a few shifts sweeping floors at the biology lab. They're the parents who ask why we're still single when their example of broken homes and sexual anarchism didn't leave us with much to go on. They're the ones who discredited the old uncomplicated patriotism and replaced it with worship of—themselves. America was a totalitarian nightmare until the advent of that holy trifecta, civil rights, women's liberation, and the gay movement: so we were taught, not by dissident faculty radicals, but by twelve years of public school classes. The rebels took over the establishment, only they wanted to keep preening like revolutionaries as they wielded power. The smugness of it was infuriating.

But as I considered the boomers more systematically, it became more important to me to sort their genuine offenses from ordinary filial resentments. Yes, the boomers benefited from an economy where a man could earn a middle-class living on a single blue-collar salary, whereas millennial couples with college degrees feel as if they both need to work full-time just to break even, but is that the boomers' fault or just the luck of the generational draw? The divorce rate spiked in the 1970s, but then it went back down. Was that brief instability the price that had to be paid for the sexual freedom we now enjoy, the inevitable overcorrection before the pendulum swung back to a happier equilibrium? Every generation since William Bradford's has thought America was going to the dogs. Then again, one of these days the Jeremiahs will be right.

That was the fundamental task in my mind as I wrote each chapter of this book. I wanted to figure out where the boomers had really departed from historical norms and done irreparable harm to Western civilization, versus where they just happened to be lucky or millennials unlucky. In the case of the two-income trap, for instance, I do think the boomers are to blame. They were the ones who hustled mothers into the workplace with the false promise that wage work was the only way to be independent and self-actualized, and that shock to the labor market killed the family wage. It was their social revolution that made two incomes practically mandatory, not abstract shifts in the economy. Divorce rates have gone down, but only because fewer people are getting married in the first place. Record numbers of millennials are reaching the age of thirty-five without ever having married. Boomers didn't just shake up the nuclear family. They broke it.

Generations are too abstract for attributions of fault and blame, so I decided to tell the boomers' story through the lives of six exemplary individuals. Looking closely at these six, I realized just how often the boomers were their own first victims. These were mainly people who would have made great contributions to humanity if they had been born at any other time. Camille Paglia, for example, would have been a gifted scholar in any century, and it is only the bad luck of having been born in 1947 that has led her to waste her talents scrutinizing pop culture. On the other hand, her insistence that Madonna is as worthy of study as Milton made it easier for subsequent generations of scholars to get their PhDs in *Sopranos* studies without ever acquiring the grounding in great literature that Paglia herself unquestionably possesses, and the rest of us now have to live with that decline in standards. None of these six boomers is altogether a villain or a victim; each one represents some aspect of the boomer tragedy in all its complexity.

Has writing this book left me more sympathetic to the boomers or less? It's difficult to say. I have a better sense of just how many aspects of my generation's disinherited condition are their fault, but I also have a better sense of what they thought they were doing when they made their mistakes. Trying to follow the thread of the boomers' misdeeds back to the original errors that produced them led me to write about many topics well beyond the usual Beatles and Bill Clinton clichés: judicial activism, imperialism, the digital revolution. The result may seem idiosyncratic. But the theme that connects all these seeming digressions is the same one that I started with, the essence of boomerness, which sometimes manifests itself as hypocrisy and other times just as irony: they tried to liberate us, and instead of freedom they left behind chaos.

Every generation is dealt its own challenges and handles them as well as it can. The boomers were dealt an uncommonly *good* hand, which makes it truly incredible that they should have screwed up so badly. They inherited prosperity, social cohesion, and functioning institutions. They passed on debt, inequality, moribund churches, and a broken democracy.

The tragedy of *Eminent Victorians* was that by the time Strachey's book was published, the figures he was attacking were all dead. He never had the chance to make them regret what he believed was their degrading effect on their country. The boomers should not be allowed to shuffle off the world stage until they have been made to regret theirs.

BOOMERS

1

THE BOOMERS

The baby boomers were born between 1945 and 1964, in the era of prosperity and self-confidence that followed America's victory in World War II. The same spirit of optimism and good fortune that boosted the birthrate in those years gave those children a lifelong sense that the world was made just for them.

Like the Victorians, the boomers have been a dominant cohort, with influence beyond the normal generational allotment. Each passing decade of the twentieth century has been defined by what the boomers were doing during it: watching TV in the suburbs in the 1950s; rocking and rebelling in the 1960s; taking things too far in the 1970s; buckling down and making money in the 1980s. This kaleidoscope of stereotyped images shows not America passing from one generation to another but a single generation moving from one phase of life to the next.

The boomers are far more self-obsessed than the Victorians were, but even if they were as humble as lambs, they would still have loomed large over the twentieth century due to sheer numbers.

Since they came of age, they have been America's largest voting bloc, the largest advertising demographic, the most important readers, drivers, diners, concertgoers. They were dominant in their youth, when their elders flattered their idealism and advertisers chased their dollars, and they clung tenaciously to their dominance for the next half century. Bob Dylan's receiving the Nobel Prize for Literature in 2016 might have made a nice capstone to this era of overwhelming boomer supremacy, the apotheosis of their global takeover, after which they might have made a graceful exit and let the younger generations have their rightful day—or late afternoon—on the cultural stage. This graceful exit has not yet been observed. The Rolling Stones will stop touring first.

Unsurprisingly, the boomers' children have grown to resent them as much as Lytton Strachey resented the Victorians. But is it more than resentment? A poll of millennials taken in 2018 found that a majority believed boomers had "made things worse" for their generation. What could they be referring to? The boomers have started no world wars, conscripted no soldiers, launched no breadlines. There is nothing in their record to compare with the pile of corpses at Passchendaele. The only fields of poppies planted on their account have been in Kandahar, not memorially.

Nevertheless, the millennials are right. The baby boomers have been responsible for the most dramatic sundering of Western civilization since the Protestant Reformation. If that is hard to accept, it is only because the boomer revolution has been so comprehensive that it has become almost impossible to imagine what life was like before it. The rise of television, for example, has altered the human mind as much as the printing press did, and one of the ways it has altered it has been to make sustained concentration virtually impossible for those raised in its atmosphere, the way a third dimension is unthinkable for the inhabitants of Flatland. The result has been generations of young people who lack a grounding in the basic facts of history, which can't possibly be absorbed by video. To cover their tracks even further, the boomers have stuffed their heirs with sufficient pseudo-knowledge to make them feel as if they know enough about the past to judge themselves superior to it.

Before the Renaissance, would-be rediscoverers of Aristotle were sometimes told by zealous churchmen that anything written before Christ was ipso facto not worth rediscovering. This is approximately how the boomers feel about themselves. Any suggestion that the Western world might not be altogether better off for their influence is immediately met with an indignant litany of all the segments of humanity who previously labored in a sad state of abject non-personhood before the boomers came along and broke their chains. So deeply ingrained is this sentiment that even the boomers' harshest critics always hasten to add their reassurances that they would not want to *undo* the least particle of the legacy of the 1960s, only temper its excesses.

I am sympathetic to this line of argument—to a point. As a woman, if I had been born in another century, my schooling might well have stopped at age twelve. On the other hand, in this age I attended some of the best schools in the world until I was twenty-one and still didn't receive an education that those benighted eras would have considered standard. Is this necessarily an improvement? In order to attempt an impartial appraisal of their legacy, it may be necessary to bracket the boomers' conversation-stopping claims to be mankind's greatest liberators for at least a preliminary moment—though this is like asking a medieval theologian to bracket the Incarnation.

Boomers have never hesitated to make themselves look better by massaging the historical record, so a good place to start an examination of their achievements is with a clear-eyed look at how life has changed in the last seventy years. People who claim to be liberators often exaggerate how bad things were before they came along, in order to make their achievement seem greater, or, in cases where their so-called liberation unleashed dark forces they did not anticipate, they pretend that things have always been this bad. Boomers do a bit of both, so it is useful to put their self-flattering narrative through a fact-check.

For all their claims to be women's greatest liberators, it would be hard to convince an impartial observer that boomer feminism has left women better off when one in five white women are on antidepressants. Feminism, for the boomers, mostly meant channeling women into paid employment on an unprecedented scale. Women have always worked, but never in American history did women outnumber men in the labor force until January 2020. Boomers promised that employment was the only way for women to be fulfilled and independent, when any socialist could have told them that there is no one more dependent than a wage worker.

You didn't have to be a socialist to guess that 1970s feminism wasn't going to work out well, just a decent observer of the psychology of the leading feminists. Betty Friedan was a self-obsessed malcontent who deliberately concealed her past as a fellow traveler of the Communist Party USA in order to make *The Feminine Mystique* seem like an honest memoir and not political propaganda. Gloria Steinem had good personal reasons for considering the nuclear family a trap. Her father was a ne'er-do-well hustler, practically a con man, and her fragile mother spent long stretches of her life institutionalized both before and after their divorce. This gave young Gloria such an abhorrence of domesticity that in her first two decades as a political organizer she never spent longer than eight days at home before setting off on the road again.

That is not how most women want to live. Friedan claimed to have been alerted to the "problem that has no name" by a 1957 Smith alumnae questionnaire that showed her fellow members of the class of 1942 languishing in suburban misery, but she misrepresented the survey's findings. It actually showed that most respondents were satisfied with their marriages, felt perfectly free to work outside the home if they wanted to (most didn't), and generally had never been happier. Polls of suburban housewives in the 1960s found that compared with their working counterparts, they were more likely to report reading widely and to feel that they were using their educations in their daily lives.

Making life easier for atypical women is a laudable goal. Florence Nightingale was an atypical woman, and even the stuffy old Victorians were grateful that she had the freedom to become eminent enough for Lytton Strachey to write about. But the net effect of boomer feminism has been to restrict the choices of typical women, taking the choice that was making most of them happy and removing it from the set of options. When married women entered the workforce in large numbers, it bid up the price of basic middle-class necessities like housing and education until, by the 1990s, families were working twice as hard to be no better off than they were when most households had a single earner. Intellectual stimulation would be small compensation for the demands of this harried lifestyle, but most of these women don't even have that. They are not journalists like Steinem and Friedan. They have jobs, not careers.

One in five white women on antidepressants, and one in six of all Americans on some kind of psychiatric medication: this would not have been possible without the boomer era's broader embrace of mind-altering drugs. It is hard to say which is sadder, the number of people who have overdosed on heroin or the number permanently fuzzying their emotional perception of the universe because they were once sad enough to pop a positive on a PHQ-9. Most depressive episodes end on their own within six to eight months; prescriptions, unfortunately for patients but fortunately for the manufacturers of Wellbutrin, last indefinitely. It is interesting to note how closely drugs have tracked the boomers as their needs and tastes have changed with age. Marijuana gave way to cocaine when they became old and rich enough to prefer "the champagne of drugs" (as *The New York Times* called it in 1974). On the legal side, the fad for Ritalin conveniently arose at exactly the right time to make the boomers' school-age children easier to manage.

This mass resort to psychotropics has been clothed in the most nauseating sanctimony, from drug dealers no less than from mental health professionals. The New Left historian Todd Gitlin insists, in his pioneering history of the 1960s, that Bay Area acid kings like Augustus Owsley Stanley III "were not in it just for the money; they kept their prices down, gave out plenty of free samples, and fancied themselves dispensers of miracles at the service of a new age." The truth is that Stanley, like a lot of silver spoon screwups, simply did not think very much about turning a profit. Others after him would. The last barrier between the dealers and the real money—Adderall money, Zoloft money—was the lingering taboo that made making money off recreational dope somehow not respectable. With the former Speaker of the House John Boehner (born in 1949) making marijuana legalization his retirement project, we may live to see the day when the street dealer's pharmacopoeia is covered by Medicaid, at which point the boomer drug revolution will be complete.

S lack-jawed, glaze-eyed, mindlessly shoveling junk food in a state of perfect passivity—no need to go to a drug den to see that, just any living room where the TV is on. The British sociologist Richard Hoggart was the first person to spot that the rise of pop culture would be a revolution in what it means to be human on par with the advent of psychology. He also spotted that it would be regressive. Instead of consuming art made by people much like themselves, the lower classes would be reduced to consuming art made by jobbing hacks catering to their audience's lowest appetites. "We are a democracy whose working people," he warned, "are exchanging their birthright for a mass of pin-ups."

Hoggart first became worried about the effects of mass culture while teaching adult education classes in Yorkshire after World War II, when he was in his late twenties—younger than many of his students, which is to say that his worries were not just fogyism. He had also grown up much poorer than any of his students, though they did not realize it until his book came out ten years later. *The Uses of Literacy* (1957) described Hoggart's upbringing in the respectable slums of Leeds, in a house too poor to afford solid meat except "a bit of rabbit occasionally." Books were as unknown as beefsteak. His grandmother, who raised him after he and his siblings were orphaned, could only just read. He knew better than to romanticize life in poverty.

Yet he could not help noticing that those unschooled slum dwellers were mentally independent in a way that his postwar students were not. His grandmother's range of cultural reference was narrow and unimpressive, consisting mainly of homespun aphorisms and the Bible, but at least her mind had not been colonized by pulp novels and Hollywood movies. The difference between the old culture and mass culture was like the difference between preparing a meal and microwaving one, and Hoggart's students had been rendered helpless in the same way as someone who has never been taught how to cook. The colonial aspect of mass culture was easier for Hoggart to spot because he was British. Mass culture, for England and Europe, was a foreign takeover. But "Americanization" homogenized the home country as much as it did the rest of the globe, sapping the life out of regional subcultures. Before the 1950s, music, theater, magazines, and even radio were all local, to one degree or another. Hollywood movies were not.

Hoggart, amazingly, was writing before the age of television, which of course came along and accelerated all the problems he was complaining about. Doomsayers saw TV as a singularly pernicious medium from the very first, and after sixty years it may be time to consider the possibility that they were right. Print took four centuries to develop mass appeal, counting roughly from Gutenberg to the *Daily Mail*. Television took fifteen years. That should be some indication of its unprecedented seductive powers. Those fifteen years happened to be the same years when the boomers were being born. From a starting point near zero in 1945, almost 90 percent of American households owned a TV by 1960. No medium has done more to shape the boomer mentality, which may be why they have been so deaf to the well-founded worries that mass-produced video is optimized to rot the human brain. They take it personally.

Assuming TV really did rot their brains, how would they be in a position to know? Its intrinsic biases—toward flash over illumination, sound bites over substance, the methods of advertising over the methods of persuasion—have become their basic intuitions. When subjective evaluation fails, objective measures must be consulted, and the most glaring objective consequence of the boomers' embrace of mass culture has been the death of both folk culture and high culture. Earlier generations felt obliged to graduate from the good-time music of their youth to opera and classical, upon reaching a certain age. Not the boomers. They believe that their adolescent taste stands in no need of improvement. Rock opera is as good as actual opera, as far as they are concerned. In 1963, the music critic for *The Sunday Times* called the Beatles "the greatest composers since Beethoven." That could be chalked up to excessive enthusiasm in the first flush of novelty. The fact that large numbers of American adults hold the same opinion fifty years later is a serious failure of taste.

During the cold war, the Communist leaders of the Eastern bloc did their best to keep pop culture out of their countries, because they believed that Western entertainment would put their children in thrall to decadent bourgeois values—and they were right. Blue jeans and rock music did more to bring down Communism than Radio Free Europe. So Honecker at least had the consolation of being vindicated. What would it take to vindicate Hoggart? If he were right, what would we see? A world where a writer for the highbrow *New Yorker* is unable to recognize a simple Gospel reference like "put out your eye if it offends you," perhaps (see Charles McGrath, "How A. E. Housman Invented Englishness," which attributes the image to Housman's own invention). One where Ivy League graduates don't know in what century the Civil War was fought (I have personally tested this). One where opponents of President Donald Trump, overwhelmed with fear for the future of the polity, reach for a name to call their movement that will convey the seriousness of our national predicament and come up with . . . Dumbledore's Army. At a certain point, the question becomes how much more evidence we could possibly need.

D rugged up, divorced, ignorant, and indebted, but at least they did it out of idealism. That has been the baby boomers' universal alibi: our intentions were good. Later, they will admit, perhaps that idealism curdled, motivation flagged, the weaker-willed sold out. Still, the original impulse was altruistic. It would be quite a blow to their self-image if it were to be discovered that the boomers' various crusades were selfish from the very beginning.

Little hypocrisies are easy enough to find, and where sex is involved, one finds little else. During a debate in 1970 over whether to introduce coed dorms at the University of Kansas, one male student said that such living arrangements would leave students "free to encounter one another as human beings." "I believe that the segregation of the sexes is unnatural," another said. "This tradition of segregation is discriminatory and promotes inequality of mankind." The same high-flown statements were heard at every school where coeducation was introduced, and they all carried the same tacit addendum: any benefit to our sex lives will be purely coincidental. From the moment the Pill became widely available, the effect of the sexual revolution has mainly been to make women more sexually available to men. This hardly even qualifies as an unintended consequence, just an unannounced one.

Women had been admitted as graduate students at elite universities like Yale since the nineteenth century. Administrators did not doubt women's capacity for higher education. It was the residential question they balked at, the idea of putting women in dormitories where alcohol and hormones would flow freely in the absence of adult supervision. When coeducation was finally accomplished, with astonishing rapidity as the first boomers matriculated, it was not because campus administrators started respecting women more or because their fears about women's sexual vulnerability had been assuaged (those fears are as valid as ever, as ongoing concerns about campus sexual assault prove). Coeducation came in because schools that did not offer a pool of sexually available females saw applications from male students dwindle and budget holes open up. "If Yale was going to keep its standing as one of the top two or three colleges in the nation, the availability of women was an amenity it could no longer do without," a modern historian of coeducation blandly records. It is hard to stifle a rueful laugh at her use of the term "amenity," which, whatever her intentions, is no more than the literal truth.

Dormitory misbehavior was a sideshow compared with the boomer sexual revolution that would have the most immediate impact on millennials, who were, in many cases, the direct result of it: the soaring out-of-wedlock birthrate. In 1960, unwed mothers were a single-digit rarity. Today, more than 40 percent of births are to unmarried mothers. The percentage of children living with both biological parents by the time the mother is forty years old is, among working-class families, 30 percent; in 1960, it was 95 percent. There are entire sections of the country where marriage has become an unattainable aspiration. Partly this is because boomers failed to give their children much in the way of helpful role modeling, and partly because millennial women have a hard time persuading their men to settle down when the bachelorhood with which they have to compete is so much more attractive, in its sexual prospects, than bachelorhood was in the days before Tinder. Naturally this revolution has had political consequences, because when fathers fail to provide, government must step in.

The boomers' most consequential political legacy may be the biggest irony of all: for all their claims to be the most progressive generation ever, the main result of the boomers' involvement in politics has been the destruction of the Left. In 1950, the Democratic Party polled fifteen points better among those without college degrees, compared with those with them. By 2016, that advantage had flipped to a fifteen-point deficit. The Labour Party in the U.K. has undergone the same transformation, from the party of the working class to the party of the college-educated elite. But if a left-wing party is no longer the party of the working class, what good is it? What *left* is it?

The great inaugurating manifesto of the New Left, the Port Huron Statement of 1962, declared existing forms of liberalism in general, and unionism in particular, to be obsolete—not a very gracious line for Tom Hayden to have taken, considering that his hosts in Port Huron were the United Automobile Workers, which allowed the Students for a Democratic Society to use their campground because one of its student leaders was the daughter of a UAW organizer. When Jack Weinberg originated the phrase "We don't trust anyone over thirty" in 1964, it was in the course of telling an interviewer that the Berkeley Free Speech Movement didn't owe anything to the radicals and Communists still kicking around California at the time. He was talking about the Old Left, not old people in general. That was the point of announcing a "New Left": to declare independence from the old kind.

The Old Left saw it coming. They had always figured that consumerism would kill socialism, and so it did. This was most obvious in Europe, where socialism was politically potent in a way it never was in the United States. The welfare state as we know it was invented by the Labour government of Clement Attlee, which inaugurated its majority by singing "The Red Flag" on the floor of the House of Commons. Then, over the following decades, the people who should have been the foot soldiers of the revolution started buying color TVs on the installment plan instead. The New Jerusalem gave way to the Macmillan boom, and even the working class started voting for the Tories because, as the PM said, they never had it so good.

In France and Germany, the generation of 1968 at least had some reason for feeling contempt for their parents' politics. It had ended in Hitler and collaboration. American boomers had no such excuse, but their contempt was if anything greater. Eugene McCarthy sneered that his primary opponent Bobby Kennedy was "running best among the less intelligent and less educated people of America." Journalist

Murray Kempton referred to the AFL-CIO as an organization specializing in "the care and feeding of incompetent white people," language one would expect to hear from a robber baron, not a self-styled populist. The AFL-CIO of the 1960s and 1970s gave its members Medicare, Medicaid, and OSHA, among other political accomplishments, and still the younger generation wrote off the old guard as backward cold-war dinosaurs.

As the boutique interests that made up the New Left eclipsed old priorities, the working class began to remember why they had organized politically in the first place: in a straight fight with the wealthy, the connected, and the articulate, they were at a decided disadvantage. In 1977, the workers at the Virgin Records plant came to the conclusion that the Sex Pistols' single "God Save the Queen" was treasonous, and they downed tools in protest. After weeks of negotiation, Richard Branson prevailed and the workers were forced to produce the record. The fact that this is remembered as a victory for free speech and not a corporate boss quashing labor is the decline of the Left in a nutshell.

The culmination of the 1960s generation's political takeover came in the 1990s, when at last they were the ones holding the highest offices. Unfortunately, this was also the moment when the working class was most in need of champions, with globalization and mass immigration both presenting problems with new urgency thanks to technological developments. Instead of champions, the working class got neoliberal triangulators like Bill Clinton and Tony Blair. By the time Hillary Clinton became the presidential nominee in 2016, there was no longer much attempt to disguise the Democratic Party's alliance with the educated and wealthy elite.

This was the year that one left-leaning news outlet ran a headline, in the wake of various business boycotts in support of progressive causes, suggesting that "corporations are replacing churches as America's conscience."

The most galling part of the boomer takeover of the Left has been that they refuse to admit they have sold out. Their remarks, even in closed-door speeches for Goldman Sachs or at billionaire meetups in Switzerland, are full of resounding liberal pieties. When Cherie Blair was confronted by a senior civil servant about the unseemliness of having used her position as Britain's first lady to arrange for thousands of pounds of discounts on designer clothes, she called upon her training as a barrister and angrily told him, "You are infringing my rights under the European Convention of Human Rights." She was referring to her right to "enjoy her possessions" without interference from the state, and she was perfectly serious.

Almost every political system in history, even the most authoritarian, has included some mechanism for the common man to make his needs heard. Kings courted their peasants to play off their nobles. Rural grandees lived close enough to their tenants and far enough from any kind of law enforcement that they had a personal interest in keeping their laborers contented. The boomers have outdone the most committed absolutist ever to sit on a throne, because they have robbed the working class of what small political power they had. They took what was supposed to be the most effective mechanism in history for guarding the rights of the disadvantaged, the left-wing parties of the Western democracies, and seized them for the wealthy and privileged. "It is a dreary old truth that those who would fight for the poor must fight the poor to do it," wrote the old Progressive Jacob Riis. It has been the genius of the boomer Progressives that they no longer bother with the first part.

The closest precedent to the boomer ethos is that of the eighteenth-century English romantics. Like the boomers, the Romantic poets were obsessed with youth. They believed that a person's opinions were worth more before they had been corrupted by any direct experience of how the world really works. They were self-indulgent both artistically and personally, with a soft spot for perception-altering drugs. It feels like something more than a coincidence that the first man who ever tried to make a living out of being an expert on the Beatles, the authorized biographer Hunter Davies, later became an expert in the Lake District and a biographer of Wordsworth.

In place of the Third World, the Romantics had France. One might have thought that England had enough liberal heroes of its own in that period, but what was the abolition of the slave trade compared with a new birth of humanity under the sign of Reason? Like the boomers and the civil rights movement, the Romantics refused to be satisfied with anything staid and incremental. Even when enthusiasm for the French Revolution took on the character of treason after the Napoleonic Wars began, they were unwilling to forswear their idealism. Disillusioning events like the French invasion of Switzerland were met more in sorrow than in anger—at least at first.

"Bliss was it in that dawn to be alive, / But to be young was very heaven!" Wordsworth forgot to mention the downside, which is that the younger you are during the revolution, the more years you have to come to regret your former opinions. That is precisely what happened to him. He eventually became not only an anti-Jacobin but an outright reactionary, opposing even the Reform Act of 1832. Robert Southey ended up writing Burkean essays for *The Quarterly Review* and Coleridge addressing long, friendly letters to the Tory prime minister explaining the metaphysical case against extending the franchise. Even Lord Byron's appetite for revolution was waning by the time he died at Missolonghi, a casualty of too much direct contact with the insufferable Shelleys and the Greek revolutionaries who, upon closer inspection, turned out to be little better than common bandits.

"Romanticism is liberalism in literature," wrote Victor Hugo, and likewise Romantics are liberals—unless they live long enough. Maybe Shelley and Keats were the lucky ones, like Jimi and Janis, like Abraham, Martin, and John, who died before their idealism had a chance to curdle.

Except that the boomers who outlived 1968 *haven't* pulled a Wordsworth. They aren't ashamed of their youthful radicalism. They are proud, inordinately proud, even of its sillier aspects. Perhaps it is because they are less reflective than the Romantic poets. Perhaps it is because the damage that they have wreaked on the world they inherited has mostly been borne by other people. Whatever the reason, the difference is not to their credit.

2

STEVE JOBS

On April 28, 2010, Jon Stewart delivered a monologue on *The Daily Show* that he said would be "more explosive than putting Muhammad in a bikini to my audience." It criticized Steve Jobs. At Apple's request, California police had just raided the apartment of a writer for the tech site Gizmodo as part of an investigation into whether the site had broken any laws when it posted photos of an unreleased iPhone 4. In fact, the prototype had been not stolen but accidentally left at a bar by an Apple software engineer. Another patron found it and sold it to Gizmodo for $5,000. The police raid came after Gizmodo had already given Apple its phone back, which was why Stewart thought the company was being unnecessarily punitive.

"Apple, you guys were the rebels, man, the underdogs. People believed in you," Stewart said. "Remember back in 1984 you had those awesome ads about overthrowing Big Brother? Look in the mirror, man!" Calling the cops on a journalist was something Bill Gates might have done, before he left Microsoft for the world of global philanthropy. "Now you guys are busting down doors in Palo Alto while Commandant Gates is ridding the world of mosquitoes? What the fuck is going on?"

Stewart was right that criticizing Steve Jobs would be controversial with his audience. *The Daily Show*'s viewership skewed educated and affluent, just like Apple's customers. Even among smartphone owners, who by definition are not poor, the iPhone is the top seller with professionals, six-figure earners, and holders of advanced degrees. The viewers watching Stewart were the people most likely to own an iPhone and also the people most likely to care whether Steve Jobs had turned into a corporate sellout.

The question of selling out, which Jobs personified for his generation, hit the boomers in their most sensitive spot. They thought of themselves as idealists, but as they grew older and their lives came to resemble their parents', it became harder for the boomers to believe that their ideals had survived the move to the suburbs. They couldn't tell themselves, as was sometimes said, that the revolution had been hijacked, because yesterday's idealists and today's sellouts were so often the same people. The guy with a Deadhead sticker on his Cadillac really did used to live on a commune before he went to law school.

This dilemma of wanting to be rebels and the establishment at the same time Steve Jobs resolved for them. In one of the first books ever written about Silicon Valley, 1985's *Big Score*, Michael Malone put his finger on Jobs's appeal to the "Woodstock generation":

> As they sat in their offices, with the dwindling mementos of their youth and their dreams, they would turn to an enormous photo of Jobs in his beard and wicked smirk

and think: "That bastard did it. He stuck by his principles and still made so many millions he can tell the establishment to kiss his ass." Then they'd get a little thrill of excitement mixed with envy. The revolution hadn't been lost after all, their lives weren't a sham.

For a generation's designated idealist, Jobs was still a conspicuous asshole. Not just when he was making money either, but even at his most hippieish. Consider his wedding cake. When he married Laurene Powell in a Zen Buddhist ceremony in 1991, Jobs served an eggless, dairyless, no-refined-sugar wedding cake that many of his guests found inedible. That proves that his vaguely mystical asceticism about food was genuine, if he wasn't willing to let it slide for a special occasion. On the other hand, forcing your friends and admirers to eat a flavorless vegan loaf is also a power trip.

That's what Jon Stewart got wrong. The idealism and the obnoxiousness were always mixed up. Whatever Steve Jobs was, he had always been that way.

Many Silicon Valley origin stories are made up by publicists, and there was an element of that to the legend of the garage. The PR maven Regis McKenna, who signed Apple as a client in 1976 before the articles of incorporation were even filed, knew from the moment the two Steves walked into his office that their story could make the company. Two all-American boys with a dream, one a gentle giant hardware prodigy, the other a Zen-inflected impresario. The slice of the market that Apple was chasing fit particularly well with Jobs's persona. Apple made computers for designers, educators, and creatives. People who just wanted to pay their taxes could buy IBM.

But the myth would not have become so iconic if it had been pure invention. Steve Jobs really was a hippie. The pilgrimage to India, the obsession with Bob Dylan, the fruitarianism—all of it was true. Ashton Kutcher tried to follow the Steve Jobs "mucusless" fruits-and-nuts diet during the filming of the 2013 biopic *Jobs*. He ended up in the hospital.

An interest in the counterculture was not so unusual for Silicon Valley, even in its earliest days. The same Stanford Research Institute team that invented the mouse also dropped acid together as a creativity exercise. John Perry Barlow came to San Francisco as a lyricist for the Grateful Dead and ended up writing for *Wired* magazine and co-founding the digital rights activist group the Electronic Frontier Foundation. His "Declaration of the Independence of Cyberspace," published in 1996, was full of 1960s phraseology ("Governments of the Industrial World, you weary giants of flesh and steel . . . you have no moral right to rule us") and inspired, among others, the young Edward Snowden. Google's first on-campus cafeteria was run by the Grateful Dead's former tour chef.

The Zelig of Silicon Valley was Stewart Brand, famous in the counterculture as founder of the *Whole Earth Catalog*. He was present at the Big Bang event of personal computing in 1968, the so-called Mother of All Demos, where Stanford researcher Douglas Engelbart debuted a machine with all the features of a modern desktop computer in rudimentary form, including hypertext and the graphical user interface. Brand was the cameraman filming the demo for posterity. He also wrote the notorious 1972 *Rolling*

Stone article about Xerox's Palo Alto Research Center that so embarrassed Xerox, by making PARC sound like a den of freaks, that
the company never marketed any of its innovations, giving up what
should have been unassailable dominance of the nascent PC industry, one of the great flubs in the history of American business. In
1985, Brand launched one of the first internet message boards, the
Whole Earth 'Lectronic Link (WELL), from which emerged such
common internet slang as "IRL" for "in real life." Several of Brand's
"WELL Beings" were old friends from his days with Ken Kesey's
Merry Pranksters.

Jobs was a little younger than Stewart Brand—whose *Whole
Earth* mantra "stay hungry, stay foolish" he borrowed for his inspira-
tional 2005 Stanford commencement address—but being a latecomer
made many people in tech all the more committed to boomer values.
Mike Murray, Apple's head of marketing in the early 1980s, put it this
way: "We all felt as though we had missed the civil rights movement.
We had missed Vietnam. What we had was the Macintosh."

For Jobs, the 1960s were never just an aesthetic. They genuinely
shaped his business. Apple was the plucky rebel in its fight against
IBM not just because of the two companies' relative sizes but because Apple stood for the principle of "one person, one computer."
Under IBM's model, individuals queued for time on a shared device
supervised by priestlike technicians. Even when IBM belatedly entered the market for personal computers, the device required hours
of introductory classes before a layman could begin to operate it.
The Macintosh you could just plug in and use. You barely needed to
look at the manual. As Jobs boasted to his friend Larry Brilliant
when the Macintosh was about to launch,

Remember in the Sixties, when people were raising their fists and saying, "Power to the people"? Well, that's what I'm doing with Apple. By building affordable personal computers and putting one on every desk, in every hand, I'm giving people power. They don't have to go through the high priests of mainframe—they can access information themselves. They can steal fire from the mountain.

Jobs's unique ability to synthesize the two sides of his personality, groovy hippie and corporate shark, is best appreciated in comparison with two colleagues who embodied only half of the magic formula. One was Jean-Louis Gassée, former head of Apple France and later VP of product development after Jobs's ouster from Apple in 1985.

Gassée, appropriately named, was famous for his pompous epigrams. He said the Apple II "smelled like infinity" and that the Apple logo conveyed "the promise of paradise." In France he had been a talk show regular, poet, spokesman for Vittel mineral water, and model for Yves Saint Laurent as well as a businessman. A French magazine once named him one of the country's best dressed men. Around the office in Cupertino, he wore leather jackets and talked in risqué metaphors ("One's experience with the personal computer should be better than the greatest orgasm"). Mac software designer Andy Hertzfeld was not alone in considering him "a total poseur." Gassée was out of the company by 1990.

The other counterexample is John Sculley, former president of Pepsi-Cola and chief executive of Apple from 1983 to 1993. He is remembered as an epically bad CEO, the man who fired Steve Jobs and brought Apple to the edge of bankruptcy. In 1986, he took the Apple advertising account away from Chiat/Day, the provocative Los Angeles agency that had made the "1984" Super Bowl ad, and gave it instead to the upbeat and orthodox New York firm BBDO, which Sculley had used at Pepsi. His signature product was the Newton, the buggy stylus-operated personal assistant that was supposed to sell a million units its first year and ended up selling only eighty-five thousand.

The knock on Sculley was that he was a bad cultural fit, the sugar-water salesman from East Coast corporate America who didn't know anything about computers. He impressed Steve Jobs during one of his job interviews by explaining how he had made Pepsi a "necktie product," that is, one the consumer proudly displays because it expresses his personality. How could any man expect to sell his vision for a necktie product in a company where nobody wears a necktie?

On the other hand, Sculley's signature accomplishment before coming to Apple was the "Pepsi Generation" ad campaign, which was specifically designed to appeal to people who *weren't* buttoned-down corporate drones. It was the quintessential campaign of 1968: According to the commercials, Coke meant stodgy and old-fashioned but Pepsi meant young, upwardly mobile, and liberated. Sculley was twenty-nine at the time, and the campaign's success made him Pepsi's youngest ever vice president of marketing. Jobs hired Sculley to help him create an "Apple generation" out of those same customers, now fifteen years older. Jobs would design the products. Sculley would be the boomer whisperer.

It should have worked. Sculley's "Pepsi Generation" sensibility, far from being overly square, should have been a good fit for Apple. So why did it fail? Perhaps because the secret of Steve Jobs's success, which allowed his hippie genius to flourish, lay in all the ways he wasn't a typical boomer at all.

When Steve Jobs was fired from Apple in 1985, he said he "felt that I had let the previous generation of entrepreneurs down— that I had dropped the baton as it was being passed to me. I met with David Packard and Bob Noyce and tried to apologize for screwing up so badly." No other boomer in Silicon Valley thought that way. They were cutting-edge capitalists for whom older generations were irrelevant and the valley was just a place.

Many things boomers love, Jobs had no time for—philanthropy, for example. He told an in-house employee Q and A in 2010 that he thought giving away money was "a waste of time." Apple never had corporate matching for charitable donations while Jobs was in charge. Bill Gates's turn to philanthropy was, for Jobs, an occasion for insult: "Bill is basically unimaginative and has never invented anything, which is why I think he's more comfortable now in philanthropy." Laurene could give her time and money to nonprofits like Teach for America. For her husband, his products were his gift to the world.

Interviewers who tried to get Jobs to talk about politics were courting frustration. "I've never voted for a presidential candidate," he claimed in 1984. "I've never voted in my whole life." He said vaguely complimentary things about Ross Perot in 1992, but only because the Texan was a major investor in his post–Apple company, NeXT. Contrast this with John Sculley, who raised money for Bill

Clinton and drafted a technology white paper for his 1992 campaign. The campaign rewarded him by leaking the improbable story that Sculley had been on the short list of vice presidential candidates before the selection of Al Gore. After winning the election, Clinton really did offer Sculley a job as deputy secretary of commerce, which he declined.

The biggest Democratic donors in California, outside Silicon Valley and Hollywood, are in the porn industry, another topic on which Jobs had very un-boomerish views. "We believe we have a moral responsibility to keep porn off the iPhone," Jobs said in 2010, explaining why the App Store had such strict rules about sexual content. "I don't want 'freedom from porn.' Porn is just fine! And I think my wife would agree," retorted Ryan Tate, editor of the *Gawker* affiliate site Valleywag. Jobs just shook his head and uttered the four most heretical words in the boomer canon. "It's not about freedom," he told Tate. "It's about Apple trying to do the right thing for its users."

The biggest difference between Jobs and his fellow boomers comes down to this: they were institution destroyers, and he was an institution builder. He told his biographer, Walter Isaacson, that he wanted "to do what Hewlett and his friend David Packard had done, which was create a company that was so imbued with innovative creativity that it would outlive them."

The compulsion to build a lasting inheritance might have been related to Jobs's complex relationship with his own heredity. His biological father was a twenty-three-year-old Syrian graduate student in political science at the University of Wisconsin who knocked up his girlfriend, a fellow graduate student, whose family urged her to give the baby up for adoption. Two decades later and at exactly the same age, Steve Jobs fathered a child with his bohemian girl-friend, Chrisann Brennan.

Being adopted was the one blighting trauma in an otherwise happy childhood. Schoolmates taunted young Steve on the playground: "What happened? Didn't your mother love you?" Co-workers wondered if adoption was the motor of his ambition. "He makes so much noise in life, he cries so loud about everything, that I keep thinking he feels that if he just cries loud enough, his real parents will hear and know that they made a mistake giving him up," one speculated. When Aaron Sorkin was commissioned to write a Steve Jobs biopic, he made Jobs's adoption the crux of the script, along with his parallel difficulties being a good parent to Lisa Brennan. Alienated from his own sense of inheritance, Jobs was driven to create something that he could pass on.

Jobs succeeded beyond his wildest hopes in building a lasting institution. Whether that is a reason to praise Jobs is uncertain; the very durability of his creation means that the rest of us now have to live in the world Silicon Valley made, a world that gives free rein to the boomers' worst vices, even the ones Jobs himself did not share.

Steve Jobs used to say that Apple was "an Ellis Island company." He meant that people too rebellious to work at Hewlett-Packard or Intel ended up there. Now the great tech behemoths are Ellis Island companies in a different way. More than half of tech workers in Silicon Valley are foreign-born. A conservative journalist once analyzed the big tech companies' spending on lobbying to see which bills received the most attention. The top targets weren't patent protections or communications spending but visas for high-skilled workers. Cheap labor from Asia is one reason wages for computer programmers have been stagnant since 1998.

Big Tech has proceeded to remake the rest of America in its image, insofar as cheap immigrant labor is the crucial ingredient that makes the app economy possible. The technology for something like online grocery delivery existed in the late 1990s. Instacart is succeeding where dot-com-bubble-era companies like Kozmo and Webvan failed because of the availability of low-wage casual labor. Kozmo's deliverymen were salaried employees with benefits. If the company had tried to hire people as contractors on 1099s in the late 1990s, it would not have found enough takers to keep the operation running.

The journalist Dan Lyons joined a tech start-up after being downsized from *Newsweek* in 2012, and the experience inspired him to write a book about how Bay Area norms have infected the American workplace, *Lab Rats: How Silicon Valley Made Work Miserable for the Rest of Us*. Nominally egalitarian but oppressive in practice, the start-up spirit insists that everyone be super psyched about their jobs all the time. No one is actually loyal to the organization in the sense of intending to work there for longer than five years, but what employees lack in commitment, they must make up for in enthusiasm. This mandatory passion is made worse by the tech industry's other contribution to the modern workplace, the smartphone. No one is ever off duty anymore. The BlackBerry's original tagline was "Always On. Always Connected." Bizarrely, this made people want to buy it.

Lyons's book focuses much of its attention on management fads like Teal, touted by its inventor as "the next stage in the evolution of human consciousness," which involves earning "badges" and consulting with "why coaches"; the Ventura-based apparel company Patagonia has used it. But California's influence runs deeper than such momentary trends. Any office where jeans are considered acceptable attire has been conquered by the spirit of the West Coast. The original Mac team that Jobs led at Apple used to wear T-shirts to the office that read "Ninety Hours a Week and Loving It." That would have been revolutionary at an East Coast company, both for its sentiment and because wearing T-shirts to work used to be frowned upon.

This low-formality, high-intensity model has been easy to get away with in Silicon Valley, full as it is of perpetual adolescents. For many years Apple had no pension plan, because none of its twenty-something employees were thinking that far ahead. When Google needed to cut benefits during the 2008 downturn, it started not by firing the masseurs or the pastry chefs but by raising the price of on-site childcare. And why not? The average age of a Google employee at the time was twenty-nine.

"Proletariat" comes from the Latin *proles*, "child," meaning it is the class that has no wealth but its offspring. Today's proletariat has had even that taken away from them. San Francisco is a city with more dogs than children. The solid middle class has been hollowed out. Paul and Clara Jobs certainly couldn't afford to live in Cupertino on a repo man's salary today. All of America's coastal cities have become playgrounds for well-credentialed meritocrats and the casual workers who serve them, and both sides of the divide are putting off marriage and kids later and later, if they have them at all.

As terrible as this economic trap is for the people stuck inside it, it is even worse for those outside. The fastest-growing jobs in America are in "wealth work," that is, the servant class for the metropolitan elite. The only thing worse than spending your adult life as a yoga instructor or dog groomer is living in a city with no one to be yoga instructors and dog groomers for.

Tech helped to create this economy, and tech is what keeps it stable by giving us the greatest bread and circuses of all time. Casino owners discovered in the late 1980s that people who gambled on screens became addicted three to four times faster than those who gambled at tables. The rest of America had learned that lesson by 1992, when a third of homes had Nintendo systems. Men without jobs have video games the way men without girlfriends have pornography, and growing numbers of men are finding the substitute good enough to be going on with, declining to pursue either permanent employment or marriage. The historian David Courtwright calls this "limbic capitalism," the redirection of America's productive energies into inducing and servicing addictions.

Peter Suderman of the libertarian magazine *Reason* has a different phrase for it. Video games mimic the process of setting goals and achieving them. Strange as it sounds, this fake achievement produces real feelings of contentment. If America's jobless can't achieve meaningful goals in the real world, he asks, why not let them have the simulacrum? Video games, says Suderman, are a kind of "universal basic income for the soul."

This is the world Steve Jobs bequeathed to us. We are all his heirs in that sense. In a more literal sense, his heir is Tim Cook, CEO of Apple since 2011.

Timothy D. Cook came to Apple from Compaq in 1998 after a long career at IBM. Though also a boomer, he was in many ways

Steve Jobs's opposite: Southern, courtly, a sports obsessive, quiet, dependable. The partnership worked because Jobs loved the way Cook took logistics off his desk and allowed him to focus on the parts of being CEO he enjoyed. Jobs could spend his time on product development and design, safe in the knowledge that Cook had the boring stuff under control.

But this unassuming figure did effect one revolution: he moved Apple's manufacturing to China. Apple had long been a holdout against outsourcing, in large part thanks to Jobs. He insisted that the Macintosh be built in America, and the operations team complied, building a factory in Fremont, California, in the East Bay. When investors in NeXT pressured Jobs to outsource manufacturing to Asia, he refused, even when Ross Perot resigned from the board in protest. There were benefits to having your engineers and your factories in geographic proximity, Jobs firmly believed, and cheeseparing wasn't necessary because his products didn't compete on price.

It was Cook who cultivated Apple's close relationship with Foxconn, the Taiwanese company that is now the largest private employer in mainland China. Foxconn was first brought on as a contract manufacturer for the iMac in 1999, and later for the iPod and the iPhone. "China weighs more in the Cook era," wrote the *Beijing News* in 2011, "in contrast to Jobs's policy to ignore China." Cook's first overseas trip as CEO was to Beijing.

Cook, like most corporate executives who moved production to Asia in the early years of the twenty-first century, insisted that the decision was driven by economic realities, but in retrospect we can see that the wish was father to the graph. Everyone said that the shift of manufacturing to Asia was inevitable, an economic no-brainer. In order to make the transfer of America's industrial base to China look like a no-brainer, one had to consider only a narrowly limited selection of quantitative measures—GDP, for example, but not American life expectancy or labor force participation—and that's assuming that only quantitative measures matter.

Utilitarian calculations, far from being objective, are the easiest moral system to manipulate to get the answer you want. When Google was deliberating in 2006 whether to enter the Chinese market despite the censorship involved, its executives performed just such a maneuver. "We actually did an evil scale," its CEO, Eric Schmidt, explained to an audience at the World Economic Forum at Davos. "We concluded that although we weren't wild about the restrictions, it was even worse not to try to serve those users at all."

(Incidentally, Jobs hated Google's style of quantitative decision making. To choose which shade of blue to put on its home page, Google tested forty-one variations to see which one got the most clicks. Jobs would have just picked one. He famously refused to look at any advance market research for Apple products, because all the data in the world is no substitute for the right stroke of intuition. "Did Alexander Graham Bell do any market research before he invented the telephone?" Jobs would say. He believed that people don't know what they want until you show it to them.)

As much as advances in shipping or communication, globalization depended on everyone's wealth being more digitized and securitized than ever before, which means that globalization is fundamentally connected to the most salient and striking economic fact about the baby boom generation: they have more debt than any other people in history. The baby boomers lived through a revolution in money. They were the first generation where everyone had a credit card, the first where everyone had investments in the stock market or a 401(k), the first generation to live in an America where finance accounts for 20 percent of GDP, that is, where one of the country's largest industries is the manipulation of debt.

This is greedy, as opposed to just fiendishly clever, because it has all been in pursuit of consumption. Debt used to be about investing. Interest was tax deductible through the 1950s because loans were almost always business expenses, intended to yield some productive return. Only in the lifetime of the boomers, and especially after their rise to financial maturity in the 1980s, was debt widely used simply for the accumulation of stuff. Fueling that appetite for consumption meant, among other things, building cheap plastic products in Asian factories.

It has been said that the baby boomers were the first generation to define themselves by what they consumed and not by what they produced. Putting advertisements for brands on one's clothes, for example, would have revolted a more dignified generation. But boomers degraded consumption as much as they elevated it. The products grew shoddier, and so did the experience of shopping. Discount giants like Target, Walmart, and Kmart—all founded in 1962—marketed themselves as stores where you could shop in your pajamas if you wanted. "If a person wants to shop in a department store, they usually cannot walk in in slacks or shorts," one discount store proprietor noted in 1961, whereas at his store shoppers wore "pedal pushers, or even dungarees."

Steve Jobs wanted to transcend this cheap consumerism by creating beautiful products as different from the usual plastic garbage as a Chez Panisse dinner is from McDonald's. In a limited way, he succeeded. He built the most beautiful products on the market, objects whose worth derived not from their rarity, as with luxury goods and status symbols, but from their intrinsic quality. But what does it say about the boomers that even their most valuable products are ones that, by their nature, will never be passed on to their children?

The other main difference between Apple under Jobs and Apple under Cook, aside from outsourcing, is that Cook has made the company political. One of his first decisions as CEO was to add an "inclusion and diversity" report to Apple's annual filings, on the model of its environmental reports. He had Apple file an amicus brief in support of Barack Obama's executive amnesty program for certain illegal immigrants, Deferred Action for Childhood Arrivals, when the Trump administration sought the Supreme Court's permission to discontinue it. For his multifarious activism, Cook has been honored with a United Nations Global Climate Action Award and a Courage Against Hate Award from the Anti-Defamation League.

The climax of Apple's shift to wokeness was Cook's coming-out, which took the form of an op-ed for Bloomberg in 2014. "While I have never denied my sexuality, I haven't publicly acknowledged it either," he wrote. "So let me be clear: I'm proud to be gay, and I consider being gay among the greatest gifts God has given me." Cook was not the first gay CEO in America. He was not even the first gay CEO of Apple Computer. That would be Michael "Scotty" Scott, who was CEO from the company's founding in 1977 until 1981, when he was fired by the board, and who in retirement has donated generously to the Seattle Opera and built up one of America's finest private gemstone collections. Cook's op-ed was nevertheless praised as an act of courage. It also served as a prelude to his donating millions of dollars to the fight to get sexual orientation antidiscrimination bills passed in Arkansas, Mississippi, and his home state of Alabama (all three bills failed).

It raises a delicate theme to suggest that being gay has shaped Cook's behavior as CEO, even though he admits as much in his op-ed ("Being gay has given me a deeper understanding of what it means to be in the minority and provided a window into the challenges that people in other minority groups deal with every day. . . . It has given me the confidence to be myself"). One would not want to give the appearance of endorsing Schumpeter's argument about John Maynard Keynes, that Keynes disdained the long term because he was gay and childless and therefore had no reason to care about the future. When Niall Ferguson mentioned this argument during a conference Q and A in 2013, it prompted such a storm of outrage that he nearly lost his job over it even after he apologized "unreservedly."

Schumpeter's argument is obviously meritless in Cook's case. Cook clearly does care about the long term. He may not want to build a better world for his children, having none, but he wants to do it for all of humanity. Of all the differences between Cook and his predecessor, that may be the greatest one of all.

The idea that men without progeny take a broader moral view, far from being a homophobic fundamentalist talking point, is the same argument the church has always made in defense of clerical celibacy. The Chinese placed eunuchs in positions of power for the same reason. Their condition removed them from the whole complex web of Confucian obligations, in order to make them more fully impartial. Palace eunuchs existed in China from the Shang dynasty to the last Qing emperor's expulsion of eunuchs from the Forbidden City in 1923, a span of three thousand years, making them perhaps the longest lasting political institution in human history. And yet far from being broad-minded, Chinese eunuchs were notoriously petty and scheming. This deliberately (and painfully) cultivated impartiality did not actually produce better results.

Though they were not exactly proponents of celibacy, transcending narrow loyalties was exactly what the baby boom generation was all about. Stewart Brand called his publication the *Whole Earth Catalog* because he thought that once humanity had seen the 1967 ATS-3 satellite photograph of Earth, the first photo ever taken of the entire planet, "no one would ever perceive things the same way." The idea came to him during an acid trip in 1966, before NASA had released the photo. Brand printed up and distributed around San Francisco hundreds of buttons asking, "Why haven't we seen a photograph of the whole Earth yet?" He put the photo on the cover of his first issue.

Imagine there's no countries it was the mantra first of the hippies, now of the globalist Davoisie. Their humanitarian universalism argues that a person who limits his loyalties to a single nation will only become narrow-minded and chauvinistic. It is a kindly sounding creed, but it simply does not work well in practice. Paradoxically, allowing everyone to be partial works out better for humanity. Steve Jobs was a family-obsessed psychological basket case haunted by themes of inheritance and lineage. Tim Cook's office contains photos of only two people, Bobby Kennedy and Martin

Luther King, and when he dies, he plans to leave his personal fortune to charity—Jobs's total opposite. But which one has done more for the world?

In a 1996 interview with *Wired*, Jobs said he had cooled on his earlier techno-utopianism precisely because he and Laurene had recently become parents. Asked which upcoming advances he was most excited about, Jobs waxed philosophical. "We're born, we live for a brief instant, and we die. It's been happening for a long time. Technology is not changing it much, if at all." Perhaps it had made him more selfish, or just more humble. Either way, he said, "Having children really changes your view on these things."

In a just world—a world of karma, as one of Jobs's Hindu sages might have put it—there would be cosmic retribution for taking Jobs's life's work and turning it to the most boomerish purposes imaginable. And so there has been. As so often happens, Big Tech's wokest boomers are being devoured by the children of the revolution.

Silicon Valley, in addition to pioneering the technologies that made globalization possible, pioneered the moral technology that sanctified it and made it sound righteous. "They see themselves as global citizens first," Eric Schmidt explained of his peers in San Francisco's post-national elite. "They're certainly patriotic about their countries and patriotic about where they grew up, and they love their mothers and so forth—but they see themselves as global citizens." *The Atlantic* quoted one American CEO as musing, "If the transformation of the world economy lifts four people in China and India out of poverty and into the middle class, and meanwhile means one American drops out of the middle class, that's not such a bad trade."

But the beneficiaries of globalization in China are most definitely *not* transcending nationalism. The highest-grossing Chinese film of all time is *Wolf Warrior II*, a 2017 action film that climaxes in a fight between the hero Leng Feng and the American mercenary Big Daddy. "People like you will always be inferior to people like me. Get used to it. Get fucking used to it," snarls Big Daddy. Leng Feng beats him to death and says over his dead body, "That's fucking history." The part of the American model that globalization was supposed to promote in China, individual liberty, hasn't materialized at all. President Clinton quipped in 2000 that China's attempt "to crack down on the internet" was "sort of like trying to nail jello to the wall." Twenty years later, it is obvious that ubiquitous smartphones have made the Chinese people less free, not more.

This has done nothing to diminish admiration for China among Silicon Valley titans like Mark Zuckerberg, who at one point proudly displayed multiple copies of Xi Jinping's book on his office shelf and even asked the premier to name his firstborn child (Xi demurred). And why wouldn't Zuckerberg admire Xi? China excels in precisely those things California can't manage to do, like keeping human feces off the street and stopping drugged-out bums from smashing car windows. Steve Jobs himself has become posthumously complicit in this China worship. Shamelessly propagandistic ads for Huawei ("Fact: Excluding Huawei from the U.S. will delay 5G deployment and adoption, reducing GDP by $104–$241 billion over six years") now regularly appear in *The Atlantic*, a magazine owned by Laurene Powell Jobs's Emerson Collective.

Meanwhile, Silicon Valley's aging boomers are discovering that their laid-back liberalism is no defense against the woke generation. In 2017, Apple's VP of diversity and inclusion, Denise Young Smith, was hounded from her job after twenty years at the company for saying that "there can be 12 white, blue-eyed, blond men in a room and they're going to be diverse too because they're going to bring a different life experience and life perspective to the conversation." (Young Smith is black.)

No company has struggled more to appease its millennials than Google, which has been forced to hire a squadron of human resources commissars just to keep the peace at the Plex. Nearly a fifth of Googlers belong to the internal discussion group "Yes, at Google," a "curated monthly newsletter of anonymized incidents of micro-aggressions and micro-corrections." "A coworker loudly exclaimed that whoever designed the cafe menu for the day must have been schizophrenic," one incident report read. "I was very relieved to see that our team member who has schizophrenia (and who sets a few desks away) was not at her desk at the time." When Google appointed Kay Coles James, the black grandmother who heads the Heritage Foundation, to an advisory board on ethics and artificial intelligence in 2019, an employee petition titled "Googlers Against Transphobia and Hate" forced the company to disband the board. The cool hippie liberalism that built Google doesn't convince the millennials who work there that their elders are well-intentioned and deserve the benefit of the doubt. It tells them they're easy marks.

There once was a CEO who died because he didn't want to be cut open. Cancer in his abdomen had progressed so far that his doctor said his internal organs "looked like the battlefield of the Marne." Surgery could have prolonged his life, but something in him rebelled against the idea, maybe deriving from a brush with health food faddism earlier in life. The situation was ironic. The last person one would expect to be afraid of medical technology was the CEO of America's biggest computer company.

That CEO was Thomas J. Watson. The founder of IBM died of stomach cancer in 1956. His son Tom junior, who had taken over as CEO one month earlier, thought his father "willed his death by refusing medical treatment." Watson senior's attitude was similar to Steve Jobs's when he missed the narrow window for lifesaving surgery after his diagnosis with a curable form of pancreatic cancer in 2003: "I really didn't want them to open up my body." Jobs wanted to try less invasive methods first, not just chemotherapy, but also treatments of his own devising involving extreme diets.

Watson and Jobs had much else in common. Before there was "Think different," there was "Think," the IBM motto that no one ever forgot because Watson put it on posters in every IBM office across the country. Watson couldn't wire a plugboard or program a punch card, but like Jobs he had a vision of the future. Both men wanted to build companies that would last. Apple didn't have songs and uniforms like IBM, but it demanded the same egoless devotion from its employees. Taking individual credit was, and is, against company culture. The institution is supposed to get the credit. If Jobs rightly belongs in the same tradition as Thomas Watson, then he was not, as everyone assumed, the first hippie CEO. He was the last of a dying breed.

" 'Revolutionize' may be the most used word in Apple advertising," one marketing department employee told the journalist Adam

Lashinsky for his book *Inside Apple*. Rebellion, more than any other concept, was the pillar of the Apple brand. The theme reached its apotheosis in a 1997 commercial that has become so identified with Jobs that a recording of it was played at his memorial service:

> Here's to the crazy ones. The misfits. The rebels. The troublemakers. The round pegs in the square holes. The ones who see things differently. They're not fond of rules. And they have no respect for the status quo. You can quote them, disagree with them, glorify or vilify them. About the only thing you can't do is ignore them. Because they change things. They push the human race forward. And while some may see them as the crazy ones, we see genius. Because the people who are crazy enough to think they can change the world are the ones who do.

Jobs's greatest rebellion was against his own generation.

3

AARON SORKIN

When President Barack Obama won reelection in 2012, his staff wondered how to handle the traditional pro forma cabinet resignations. They knew that each cabinet secretary was supposed to submit a letter of resignation as a matter of courtesy, in order to give the president the option of shuffling his cabinet without the burden of having to fire anyone, but no one knew the exact protocol. Are the letters submitted on Inauguration Day, or on January 1, or at the secretaries' individual convenience? Are any other department heads traditionally included? The White House cabinet secretary at the time, Chris Lu, asked his staff to look up the relevant precedents.

They discovered that the tradition did not exist. "Those of us who were thinking about this question had a feeling that the cabinet was supposed to submit their resignations, and we did some research and we couldn't find anything," Lu recalled. "At that moment, we realized we all must have been thinking about this episode of *The West Wing* where Leo asks for the cabinet resignations." Lu is referring to season 4, episode 10, which features the first full cabinet meeting after President Bartlet's reelection, during which Chief of Staff Leo McGarry does indeed request letters of resignation from everyone by the end of the business day.

The majority of White House staffers at the time, and the majority of staffers on the Hill, were under thirty (Lu himself was forty-six years old). Someone in their late twenties when Barack Obama was elected would have been exactly the right age to have watched *The West Wing* in high school or college, just as they were figuring out what they wanted to do with the rest of their lives. In the ten years since 2008, which also happened to be the year I graduated from college, I have seen familiar faces from the Yale Political Union climb the ladder at the Justice Department, Booz Allen Hamilton, Vox Media, and the Democratic Party, and I can personally confirm what must be, to people living outside Washington, a disturbing truth: a significant portion of our ruling class is made up of former *West Wing* obsessives.

Aaron Sorkin has expressed some bashfulness about this. He never meant to be pied piper to a generation of political operatives. His college major was musical theater. The *sound* of intellectual debate is what animates him, he insists, not the issues. "I want to be really clear about this: I am not particularly politically sophisticated," he always tells interviewers. "If I have a talent, it's a phonetic talent."

There is no reason Sorkin should feel especially guilty. One in three Americans told a Kaiser survey that the show *ER* helped them make health-care choices, and one in five doctors say they have had patients ask them about diseases and treatments they've seen on prime-time TV. Applications for residencies in emergency medicine surged after *ER* went on the air. It's just the sort of thing that happens with television shows, even ones that make *The West Wing*'s idealized depiction of politics look like cinema verité.

His viewers are the ones who should feel ashamed of themselves. Contrary to his protestations, Sorkin is not an idiot savant. His flair for dialogue is connected to a real critical intelligence. He may not know anything about politics, but on the subjects he knows, his opinions reflect the same old-fashioned virtues as his characters: integrity, seriousness, imagination, brains.

The subject Sorkin knows best is the entertainment industry. It is his home industry, and has been for two generations. His father was a copyright lawyer for Warner Bros. who commuted into Rockefeller Center from suburban Scarsdale for forty years. Sorkin's first show, *Sports Night*, was about television. When *The West Wing* made him the hottest TV screenwriter in town and he had the freedom to write basically whatever he wanted, he did two more shows about television: *Studio 60 on the Sunset Strip*, about a *Saturday Night Live*–type sketch comedy show, and *The Newsroom*, about a cable news show.

Both shows flopped. Critics called them pompous. How ridiculous to write with such high-flown moral seriousness about late-night comedy, everyone said. Lighten up, it's not the White House. The irony was that, for once, Sorkin wasn't speaking loftily just for the sound of it. He truly believes that decisions of television executives and producers mean more, to more people, than the decisions of politicians. Between the end of *The West Wing* and the beginning of *Studio 60*, Sorkin wrote a play called *The Farnsworth Invention*, a three-act drama about the invention of the television. Near the end of the play, the New York radio mogul David Sarnoff is about to steal the crucial cathode ray projection patent from the Mormon college dropout Philo Farnsworth. Sarnoff explains to his wife why controlling the future of television is so important:

> It's gonna change everything. It's gonna end ignorance and misunderstanding. It's gonna end illiteracy. It's gonna end war.

> *How?*

> By pointing a camera at it.

That is how Aaron Sorkin feels about television, and he has been thoroughly vindicated—not his idealism, but his grasp of television's raw power to influence millions of people and change the course of history. Who did more to make gay marriage a reality, Barack Obama or the creators of *Will & Grace*? If you send the Obama speechwriter Jon Favreau and Katie Couric into a Starbucks, which one will get mobbed by fans? To this day, there are people who don't realize that it was Tina Fey, and not the real Sarah Palin, who said, "I can see Russia from my house!"

It's an agonizing irony: television made people care about Sorkin, but Sorkin couldn't make people care about television. Viewers liked *The West Wing* because it sounded serious, and Sorkin tried to explain that he didn't actually know what he was talking about. Then he got serious about something he did know something about, and everyone told him to lighten up. Baby boomers love idealism, but do they even know the difference between the real thing and the imitation? Is their appreciation of moral integrity real or just an affectation? Aaron Sorkin found out the hard way.

On January 17, 1998, two things happened: Aaron Sorkin finished the pilot script of *The West Wing*, and Matt Drudge hit publish on the story that President Bill Clinton had had sex in a room adjoining the Oval Office with a twenty-three-year-old intern. An unpropitious time to be shopping a series about heroic White House staffers, you might think. In fact, Monica Lewinsky was *The West Wing's* salvation. The scandal allowed the executives at NBC to tell Sorkin that they wanted to wait a year before making a decision, to give America time to stop giggling. This was not really what they wanted to do. They wanted to turn him down flat.

Don Ohlmeyer was the head of NBC West Coast at the time, and he was not the kind of executive to give highbrow pitches a sympathetic ear. He came up producing sports shows like *Monday Night Football*. In the entertainment division, his creative interventions had included forcing Lorne Michaels to fire Chris Farley and Adam Sandler because he didn't think they were funny and having Norm MacDonald taken off "Weekend Update" for making too many jokes about his old friend from the Buffalo Bills, O. J. Simpson.

Ohlmeyer had also insulted Sorkin personally in the pages of *The New Yorker*. Sorkin's first show, *Sports Night*, was then running on ABC, and the *New Yorker* article described his battles with the network over, among other things, the cheesy laugh track they had added to make the show feel more like a sitcom. Ohlmeyer is quoted as the head of a rival network, mocking Sorkin's purism:

"I'd love for the show's creators to prevail on the laugh track—it would improve the chances for our show in that slot. Nobody's coming home from work saying, 'Gee, I can't wait to see that new show without the laugh track'—that's just creative caca. So what makes Aaron think he's so right?"

This was the man to whom Sorkin had to pitch *The West Wing*. Thankfully, by the time the yearlong waiting period had elapsed, Ohlmeyer was no longer at NBC. His replacement was much more simpatico. He did not, as Ohlmeyer's team had, suggest that Sorkin punch up a story line about stranded Cuban refugees by having Bradley Whitford's character swashbuckle down to Miami and captain the rescue ship himself. Instead, he gave Sorkin the green light and left him alone to make the show his own way.

The first five minutes of *The West Wing* would never work if they were aired today. It introduces each of our main characters by showing them receiving a message—by phone, on their pager, from an airline stewardess relaying a note patched up to the cockpit— saying, "POTUS was in a bicycle accident." The joke is that the civilians passing the message along don't understand it. "Tell your friend Potus he's got a funny name," says the girl Sam Seaborn wakes up next to. Nowadays, every housewife in Boise knows the acronym POTUS, and FLOTUS and SCOTUS, too. An oral history of the Obama White House published in 2018 felt it necessary to footnote only "ROTUS," which stands for "receptionist of the United States."

The late 1990s were a less sophisticated time. There had never been a TV show about political staffers. Political staffers themselves were a fairly new phenomenon. The first president to have a pollster in his inner circle was Jimmy Carter with Pat Caddell (later a *West Wing* consultant). The first rock star staffers were George Stephanopoulos and James Carville, made famous by the campaign documentary *The War Room* (1993). The American Association of Political Consultants, founded in 1969, didn't induct the first honorees of its AAPC "Hall of Fame" until 1991. Karl Rove, Roger Ailes, Lee Atwater, Stan Greenberg—from consultants to pollsters to self-styled "strategists," the entire profession is a boomer creation.

These adjuncts of the political process arose out of broader changes in American democracy that coincided with the rise of the boomers. As the state grew larger and more intrusive, governing became more technocratic. Lawyers and businessmen gave way to economists. Every aspect of politics became more specialized, the campaign side no less than the side devoted to governing. Around the same time, higher education was undergoing its meritocratic revolution, which meant that Harvard and Yale stopped producing gentlemanly amateurs and instead unleashed on the rest of the country class after class of ambitious strivers who believed that hard work and intelligence could solve any problem. After Clinton was inaugurated, Washington old-timers felt that his team brought a whole new approach to government: younger, fresher, wonkier. What they were detecting was the transition to rule by boomer meritocrats.

The rise of this technocracy left a void. As the 1968 Sorbonne protesters chanted, "You can't fall in love with a growth rate." That was the hole that *The West Wing* filled. Sorkin took plotlines about things like the decennial census and invested them with moral drama, with no trace of irony or cynicism. A class of people too wonky to be glamorous, and too young to have gravitas, were made to look heroic. The show didn't correct popular misconceptions about White House staffers. There *was* no popular conception of White House staffers. It created one.

How has this worked out for the rest of us? Leave aside for the moment the civilians watching at home. What has been the effect on people who went into politics because of, or even just concurrently with, the popularity of the show? Chris Matthews once said that the problem with Washington was that "you can't measure outputs. You measure input. This is a town where the GNP is government. And government is measured not by output but by how many hours you put in. Everybody says, 'I've been really busy this week. Are you busy? I've been busy. I must be busy.' It's like busy-ness is a value in itself." *The West Wing* romanticized this mentality, showing characters who sleep in their offices, give up their personal lives, break up their marriages, for the sake of the cause.

All things being equal, it is better for a political class to be hard-working than not, but by turning devotion to work into a fetish, Sorkin encouraged D.C. staffers to think of themselves as a caste apart. Well-intentioned, hypercompetent, with the relevant facts at their fingertips at all times, these were just the sorts of people anyone would want to see running their country. In the absence of a strong preexisting commitment to small government, one could easily come to the conclusion that such people ought to have as much power as they can get their hands on. Sorkin taught a generation of Washingtonians that they were capable of running the country from eighteen acres on Pennsylvania Avenue if only they put in the hours and, worse, that they deserved to.

The nice thing about a fictional universe is that all problems really do have solutions. *The West Wing* never hesitated to tweak the facts to make things easier for its protagonists or to give them a happier ending. When President Bartlet faces a Rwanda-like genocide in Africa, he dispatches the military intervention that Clinton, to his everlasting regret, did not. When Bartlet intervenes to reinstate the democratically elected president of Haiti, the Haitian leader does not turn out to be a mentally unstable murderer as Jean-Bertrand Aristide unfortunately proved to be. When the character played by Rob Lowe accidentally uses a phrase from Mao's *Little Red Book* in a speech, his boss catches it right away, as opposed to the phrase from the *Communist Manifesto* ("all that is solid melts into air") that made it through ten drafts of Clinton's 1996 State of the Union before an intern recognized it.

The gap between reality and fantasy is widest in the character of the president himself. Faithful husband, devout but tormented Catholic, New Englander, economics professor, President Josiah Bartlet is in many ways Bill Clinton's photo negative. He shares some of the real-life president's virtues but completely lacks his appetites, and appetitiveness was, after all, President Clinton's defining quality. His libido was the least of it. At meetings where the White House kitchen set out enough breakfast pastries to feed a conference table, Clinton was notorious for eating the whole plate himself. Strobe Talbott's school-age children nicknamed him "the guy who eats all the ice cream," because that's just what he would do as governor of Arkansas when he stayed with the Talbotts on trips to D.C. He was a glutton for everything—attention, love, carbohydrates.

One of the plotlines in the third season of *The West Wing* is the debate among President Bartlet's advisers over whether he should apologize to the country for concealing during the campaign that he has multiple sclerosis. This was inspired by the debate within the Clinton camp about whether his speech coming clean about the Lewinsky affair should include an explicit apology. In the end, the speech Clinton gave on August 17, 1998, included the phrases "lapse in judgment," "personal failure on my part," "take complete responsibility," and "deeply regret," but not "I apologize."

On *The West Wing*, President Bartlet does apologize—to his staff. "It occurs to me, I never said I'm sorry. I am. For the lawyers, for the press, for the mess, for the fear," he tells them backstage before he goes out to give the speech launching his reelection campaign (which may or may not include a public apology; it is not specified). President Clinton also eventually apologized, publicly, once the polls taken in the wake of his August speech made it clear that the American public would accept nothing less. But when Betty Currie sat down with interviewers from the Presidential Oral History Project in 2006 to record for posterity her recollections of her eight years as Clinton's personal secretary, she was asked at one point to describe the grand jury deposition she gave during the Lewinsky affair:

> They kept asking me questions about people and at one point I told them, "I cannot mention another name to you because as soon as I mention a name, you subpoena these young kids who can't afford any lawyers. Now ask me what you want, but I'm not saying any other names." I just couldn't do it anymore.
>
> *Did you ever have a subsequent conversation with the president about your ordeal through this?*

We never talked about it.

So there was never an apology from him.

Never an apology.

This is the side of the Clinton White House that never shows up in *The West Wing*, the side that is self-indulgent, narcissistic—boomerish.

Sorkin himself is so old-fashioned that he almost doesn't qualify as a boomer at all. He first came to Hollywood's attention when his play *A Few Good Men* opened on Broadway in 1989. No one comes to Hollywood by way of the East Coast stage anymore. He says he kept pop culture references out of *The West Wing* so that the show wouldn't feel dated in six months, but one gets the impression that the real reason was that he thinks pop culture has been all downhill since Gilbert and Sullivan. Oddly, considering how highly boomers regard their cultural ephemera, it's his very old-fashionedness that makes Sorkin such boomer catnip. In the same way that boomer spirituality is parasitic on the religious institutions that supply the divine buffet, boomer idealism is parasitic on people who believe in something enough to make sacrifices for it, who don't just like the idea of believing in something. Such people almost always have one foot in the pre-boomer era.

s *The West Wing* a liberal show? The objection has been voiced. Sorkin admits that when Ronald Reagan won the 1984 election, when he was twenty-three years old, he did not know a single person who had voted for him, and neither his milieu nor his personal politics have gotten more conservative since then. On the other hand, when *A Few Good Men* became a hit on Broadway, Sorkin was approached by countless people asking him about his military background. They assumed, from the play's obvious appreciation for honor and loyalty to Corps, that the playwright would be a hard-bitten marine general in retirement. This was a testament to Sorkin's creative powers. Unfortunately, it also gave him the idea that he was some kind of red state whisperer, perfectly positioned to make the two sides of the culture war comprehensible to each other again.

In theory, this was a reasonable ambition for Sorkin, and certainly one well suited to his talents. His superpower after all is making people talk to each other, and that is what the opposing sides of the culture war most need to relearn how to do. Again and again, Sorkin has written Republican characters into his TV shows, not as villains, but as well-intentioned foils for his own liberal mouthpieces: Ainsley Hayes and Cliff Calley in *The West Wing*, Harriet Hayes in *Studio 60*, Will McAvoy in *The Newsroom*. After so many attempts, we can now say with certainty there are no conservatives in Hollywood, because if there were, at some point surely one of them would have tapped Sorkin on the shoulder and told him sorry, buddy, you still haven't got us right.

Let no one say Sorkin has not tried to be fair. He hired Peggy Noonan and Marlin Fitzwater, Bush 41's press secretary, as consultants on *The West Wing*. Most of the communication between Sorkin and his writing staff on the show took the form of so-called pro-con memos, where Eli Attie (former Al Gore speechwriter) or Lawrence O'Donnell (former Pat Moynihan chief of staff, current

MSNBC host) or whoever would summarize their position on some issue that they cared about and then give the counterarguments of a smart person who disagreed with them. This excellent system was responsible for the show's evenhanded treatment of such issues as farm subsidies, teachers' unions, and the Equal Rights Amendment. However, his conservative characters always saved their best Sorkinesque monologizing for their fellow Republicans—Ainsley Hayes calling a congressional negotiator a "schmuck," or Cliff Calley accusing a GOP congressman of "killing the party" by making a public issue of the White House chief of staff's past alcoholism.

The most misbegotten of Sorkin's right-wing characters was Harriet Hayes of *Studio 60*, which is odd because she is the one based on a real person. In 2005, Sorkin began dating Kristin Chenoweth, the actress with an opera-grade voice who originated the role of Glinda in *Wicked*. A love of Broadway theater was about the only thing they had in common. Chenoweth is an evangelical Christian from Oklahoma who records gospel albums and doesn't mind talking about Jesus in interviews. In 2006, Sorkin decided to make a relationship very similar to theirs the dramatic spine of the much-anticipated follow-up series to *The West Wing*. *Studio 60 on the Sunset Strip* would feature an on-again, off-again romance between Matt Albie, the head writer of the show within a show, and Harriet Hayes, its God-fearing leading lady. This was not vanity. In a politically polarized country, Sorkin thought such a relationship could have a deeper meaning. "Half of this country hates the other half," one character tells Albie, but "for ninety minutes a week, you and Harriet come together."

The problem was that the real-life Chenoweth is not a conservative. A self-described "liberal Christian" and "swinger when it comes to voting," her politics are broadly similar to Sorkin's on just about every issue not involving the divinity of Jesus Christ. That meant that when a script required Harriet Hayes to present the conservative position on something like gay marriage, Sorkin had to wing it. Unfortunately, his idea of what a hypothetical Christian would say when asked why discrimination against gays wasn't equivalent to discrimination by race was not very accurate. "Black people had lived openly as black people for four hundred years before civil rights. For four hundred years. Gay people have lived openly for about thirty," Harriet says. "How about giving the rest of the world a little time to catch up?" If a consultant for *The West Wing* had been that lazy in his pro-con memo, he would have been fired. It is unfortunate that Peggy Noonan was not available to consult on *Studio 60*.

The knock on *Studio 60*, besides that it was overwritten, was that it was unrealistic. Sketch comedy writers don't spend days agonizing about the effect of their jokes on American democracy, critics said. They don't stick with highbrow sketches that get zero laughs out of a commitment to artistic integrity. The network suits who are their bosses—played on *Studio 60* by Amanda Peet and Steven Weber, two of the best actors of all the series regulars Sorkin has ever had—don't turn down reality TV shows for being too tawdry, or refuse to negotiate with the FCC over the appropriate fine to pay for broadcasting a soldier saying "fuck" on a live news segment out of commitment to the principle that war coverage must never be censored.

Actually, sometimes they do, as Sorkin himself had reason to know. While he was at NBC making *The West Wing*, Scott Sassa (Ohlmeyer's successor) really did wake up one morning and decide, for no other reason than to satisfy his own conscience, that the network had to drop the upcoming reality show *Chains of Love*, even if it meant losing the money they'd already spent to win the bidding war for it. The show involved shackling a woman to four different men to determine which one she wanted to date. The years *The West Wing* was on the air happened to be a particularly interesting time in network television, and of all the networks NBC was the most interesting place to be, as the last holdout against reality TV as practiced by Mark Burnett and his epigones. Should the network ignore "unscripted TV" and take the ratings hit until the fad went away, or try to do reality shows in a classier way consistent with the network's reputation, or just embrace the revolution and copy the latest midget-toss show from Fox? Sorkin was around when NBC's executives were having this debate, and believe it or not, the network's responsibility to its viewers and its legacy of quality programming were part of the conversation.

Nor is late-night sketch comedy as immune from idealistic self regard as Sorkin's critics alleged. The Saturday after the 2016 election, which also happened to be the week that Leonard Cohen died, Kate McKinnon opened *Saturday Night Live* by performing a somber, joke-free rendition of his ballad "Hallelujah" alone at a piano, dressed all in white and made up to look like Hillary Clinton. Before handing off to the main titles, she looked into the camera and said with bottomless sincerity, "I'm not giving up, and neither should you." Among the many entertainment bloggers and Twitter celebrities who thanked McKinnon for bringing America together for a much-needed moment of healing were doubtless some of the same people who had accused Sorkin of taking *SNL* too seriously.

The real false note in *Studio 60* was its depiction not of comedy writers or network executives but of evangelical Christians. The Harriet character was only the beginning. The show also featured a reporter from the fictional magazine *Rapture* who organizes a boycott of *Studio 60* over a sketch called "Crazy Christians" (nature of sketch never specified) and a game show sketch titled "Science Schmience!" that mocks the contestant "Cora Rae from Liberty Bible College" over the supposedly widespread Christian belief that hurricanes are caused by "secularists eroding God's protective shell over America." Sorkin devotes an entire episode—actually a two-parter—to Matt Albie's effort to circumvent the network ban on certain swear words by writing a sketch where Jesus is a character. "Jesus Christ, it's hot in here" isn't an expletive if the guy who says it is actually addressing Jesus Christ, get it?

As it happens, devout Southern Baptist comediennes are not unprecedented on *Saturday Night Live*. Victoria Jackson, the baby-voiced blonde who was a cast member from 1986 to 1992, attended Florida Bible College and used to watch *The 700 Club* every morning. (By contrast, when Kristin Chenoweth got in trouble with her gay fans for going on *The 700 Club* to promote her gospel album in 2005, she told them she had never watched the show and didn't know much about Pat Robertson except that he was a pastor.) Sorkin might have benefited from lifting plot ideas from the real-life conflicts that arose between Jackson's beliefs and her job—except that there weren't any. She once had to tell Lorne Michaels that she wouldn't pretend to pray as part of a sketch, but apart from that she took everything they threw at her, including a blasphemous appearance by the guest host Sam Kinison. "I still went to work, because my contract wasn't based on, 'I come to work if I approve of the host,'" Jackson said. The only *SNL* cast member in her day to boycott an episode for moral reasons was Nora Dunn in 1986, on left-wing feminist grounds, when the guest host was Andrew Dice Clay.

As for stupid network strictures, they are as old as television itself and by no means a monopoly of Christians. General Motors once sponsored a historical drama about the assassination of Abraham Lincoln but forbade the writers to mention the name of the theater in which the event took place, for fear of giving free advertising to Ford. In 1959, the National Gas Association asked that *Playhouse 90*'s production of *Judgment at Nuremberg* refrain from mentioning "gas" in any negative context having to do with Nazi death camps. Product placement is worth millions to advertisers because they know that even half a second of visibility can have a major impact on consumer awareness when broadcast over a mass medium. If television executives sometimes get touchy about seemingly minor details, it's only because they know the same thing about their medium's vast power.

The religious Right is simply a bête noire of Sorkin's. It goes as far back as *Sports Night*, which featured a multi-episode arc about the main character using his sports show to go after Jerry Falwell. The pilot of *The West Wing* revolves around whether Josh Lyman will get fired for making a snide remark to a female evangelical on a Sunday talk show. His job is saved when, at the climactic meeting between Josh and his colleagues and the evangelical virago and hers, she makes the gaffe of referring to Josh's "New York sense of humor." "She was calling us New York Jews," says the White House communications director, Toby Ziegler, indignantly. "When she said 'New York sense of humor,' she was talking about you and me."

Just how disconnected this scenario was from reality can be seen in a weird blip of a news story from the 2016 Republican presidential primary. Senator Ted Cruz accused the front-runner, Donald Trump, of embodying "New York values," and outlets from CNN to *The New Republic* leaped to ask whether Cruz's remark was anti-Semitic, even though Trump is of German heritage and Cruz was quick to explain that his remark had no coded meaning aside from the immediately obvious one that "the values in New York City are socially liberal, are pro-abortion, are pro-gay marriage." Everyone who had seen the *West Wing* pilot understood what was going on; those who had not seen it were baffled.

The poor reception of *Studio 60* made it clear that the average American viewer is simply not as passionate about television qua television as Aaron Sorkin is. The solution was obvious: find a way to combine the idealism about politics that drew people to *The West Wing* with the idealism about television that gets Sorkin's blood moving. As if by mathematical formula, his next series was a workplace drama about a nightly cable news program, originally called *More as This Story Develops* and later retitled simply *The Newsroom.*

The show features Jeff Daniels as the star anchor of *News Night* and Emily Mortimer as his executive producer, whose job of coaxing her anchor into doing the right thing every episode is made easier by the fact that she is his ex-girlfriend and he is in love with her. Together they rededicate the show to an ethos of "speaking truth to stupid" that they refer to as their "mission to civilize," to the annoyance of the network's corporate bosses who liked it better when their flagship anchor did not pass up five minutes with Lady Gaga in order to do an exposé on the debt ceiling. The third episode begins with an on-air editorial of 757 words, longer than the average newspaper op-ed, announcing that *News Night* will no longer be driven by ratings but by "the simple truth that nothing is more important to a democracy than a well informed electorate." Those five minutes and twenty seconds of Jeff Daniels talking into a camera, reciting his lengthy manifesto, end with his saying, "Who are we to make these decisions? We're the media elite."

Strangely, Sorkin chose to make the Daniels character a Republican who nonetheless spends all his time inveighing against the Tea Party as "the American Taliban." "I'm a registered Republican," he explains. "I only seem liberal because I believe that hurricanes are caused by high barometric pressure and not by gay marriage." Unceasing war against the supposed radicals who have hijacked his party becomes a central part of the "mission to civilize." Alas, as with Harriet in *Studio 60*, the dialogue Sorkin writes for his Tea Party punching bags falls short of verisimilitude. One talking head explains his opposition to gay marriage by saying, in reference to HIV/AIDS, "Normal, God-fearing heterosexual couples don't spread those kind of diseases." No one polished enough to appear on television has ever begun a sentence with the phrase "Normal, God-fearing heterosexual couples" except in sarcasm. In episode 9 of the first season, Sorkin has a plotline where Christian vandals spray-paint BABY KILLER on a character's window—in Manhattan!—after she goes on *News Night* and utters some tepidly pro-choice remarks. His Baptist-phobia had advanced to the point of delusion.

Ideology aside, the tragedy of *The Newsroom*—which was a commercial failure for all three seasons that HBO gave it—was that in the course of trying to do a show about something he loved, Sorkin ran smack into two things he absolutely hates: the internet and journalism. Sorkin's contempt for the internet is long-standing and well attested. In addition to the oblique swipes implied by his love for "the media elite," his shows are peppered with explicit references to online journalism as "the pajama people" whose exemplary practitioner "has a freezer full of Jenny Craig and is surrounded by her five cats." These insults date back to the early days of *The West Wing* when, perhaps not coincidentally, Sorkin had a bad experience with the online message board Television Without Pity. Sorkin posted a few times under the pseudonym Benjamin and quickly became embroiled in some unenlightening flame wars that embarrassed NBC, which was forced to forbid its star showrunner to go on the site again.

Whatever conclusions Sorkin drew from that brush with the internet's dark side were amply confirmed over the next two decades by the likes of *Gawker*. Mainstream media outlets were forced by competition from unscrupulous online sites, and by their own shrinking budgets, to lower their journalistic standards. By the time of the Sony hack, when private emails from the Sony Pictures film studio were leaked to the press, there was not much chance that establishment newspapers and networks would take the high road. Sorkin nevertheless fired off a *New York Times* op-ed in protest, arguing that self-respecting media outlets should never have touched emails that were obtained illegally and had no news value apart from the embarrassment they caused Hollywood big shots. In 2012, when Sorkin snapped at a female journalist during a Q and A session, "Listen here, internet girl, it wouldn't kill you to watch a film or read a newspaper once in a while," it was hard to tell who felt more vindicated, those who thought Sorkin was a misogynist or those who considered him a net-phobic fuddy-duddy.

Sorkin himself might have benefited from picking up a newspaper or a book when he was writing *The Newsroom*. If he had, he would have known that attempts to improve TV news are nothing new. When the movie *Network* came out, the head of the CBS affiliate in Los Angeles, Van Gordon Sauter, distributed copies of Howard Beale's impassioned rant to everyone at the station. Flash forward six years and Sauter was president of CBS News and a byword for dumbed-down, sensationalized coverage. "Tax policy had to compete with stories about three-legged sheep, and the three-legged sheep won," Bill Moyers said of the Sauter era, shortly before he quit in disgust. Sauter's good intentions had run afoul of hard realities like budget limitations and ratings. "No matter who was sitting in my chair, the same steps would have been necessary," he said at the end of his tenure in 1986. "You can change the players, but let me assure you, you don't change the rules."

There is no denying that network news will never return to the golden age of Murrow and Cronkite. The only question is when the decline became irreversible. It might have been the early 1980s, shortly after Cronkite's retirement, when in the blink of an eye all three networks were bought by corporate parents that suddenly started expecting their news divisions to earn a profit. Before NBC became a subsidiary of General Electric, it was always understood that its news division, like the other networks', would be subsidized by the rest of the company as a public service. One could locate the decisive moment a decade later, with the advent of twenty-four-hour cable news, or a decade after that, with the rise of the internet. Whatever date one picks, none of the turning points quite correspond to Sorkin's critique, which is more comprehensive.

Sorkin's standards for what qualifies as good news are impossibly high, so high that it is not clear that even Murrow or Cronkite met them. He has his *Newsroom* heroes refuse to cover the Anthony Weiner sexting scandal because they think his constituents should only care how he votes. They turn down an exclusive on General David Petraeus's resignation because the story, while juicy, doesn't "provide any information the voters should have before they cast a ballot." In *Studio 60*, there is a tense scene between Amanda Peet's character and an entertainment reporter who has been writing gossipy stories about her supposed unpopularity and incompetence. When the reporter asks her about "talk among people in the industry" that she is about to be fired, she accuses him of ginning up the very rumors he is supposedly covering. "Stories need conflict, that's understandable, except reporters aren't supposed to be storytellers. Stop trying to entertain me."

Taking real people's lives and turning them into entertainment for strangers is indeed dubious, but that is what journalism is. It might come as a shock to Sorkin, but even eat-your-vegetables stories about budget projections need good guys and bad guys in order to hold the reader's interest. *The Newsroom* mocks campaign coverage as stenography, but what are journalists supposed to do? It would take a whole career spent on one topic for journalists to be able to independently assess what their sources told them about it, and even when journalists are able to do that, they can't make the public care. It is not cravenness or greed on the part of news directors that prevents them from providing the pristine, well-informed, and civic-minded coverage of Sorkin's fantasies, but the unavoidable limitations of journalists and the preferences of their audience.

CBS News went through a crisis of morale in the years after Walter Cronkite handed the chair to Dan Rather. Cable was cutting into its revenue, corporate raiders like Ted Turner were circling the company, and the former "Tiffany Network" was losing its sense of mission. During the worst of it, Dan Rather one day began ending every broadcast of the *Evening News* with the word "Courage." Everyone was baffled (especially on the one occasion when the Texan switched it up and said "Coraje") and asked him what the meaning of the new sign-off was. Alas, presented with the opportunity to give a rallying cry to his dejected troops, Rather whiffed and simply said that "courage" was one of his favorite words, like "meadow." He dropped it after a few weeks. Sorkin has less of an idea of what makes a good news broadcast than Rather ever did. He doesn't even seem to like journalism at all. *The Newsroom* was a reasonable effort to recapture the idealism that made *The West Wing* a success by returning to the world of politics, but in the absence of any feeling for the world he was trying to depict, Sorkin sounded like he was just saying his favorite words.

It has been only twenty years since *The West Wing* went on the air, and already the forces that seemed so fresh and new in the Clinton era have reached the point of decadence. Politics is more dominated by language than ever, but it turns out that the logical culmination of the reduction of politics to communications is not gladiatorial battles between dreadnoughts of Sorkinian eloquence but Jen Palmieri. The leading Democratic communications professional of her time—former White House director of communications, top press guru for Hillary Clinton's 2016 campaign—is aggressively *inarticulate*. She can hardly get out a sentence. Half of her meaning is expressed in eye rolls and facial expressions. One journalist for *The New York Times* couldn't understand why her transcripts of Palmieri always looked like "It's, um, I don't, I don't, we would, uh, it is, uh, I just saw the president's, um, uh, comments, about it" and "Like, we have a plan, literally," until it hit her: it was a way of rendering herself unquotable. John F. Kennedy used to do the same thing for the TV cameras—give short, punchy answers to questions he liked and long, rambling answers to questions he didn't.

The technocrats who were insurgents under Clinton are now the establishment. The economists have cemented their lock on power, their expertise too terrifyingly advanced for lesser mortals to question. There are no longer any alternative centers of power to the financial wizards with their graphs and projections, no countervailing force to balance their enormous influence. When the public's exasperation reached a breaking point in 2016, they had no champions within the existing power structure to turn to and so had no choice but to toss out the establishment in its bipartisan entirety.

Meanwhile, the public is more sophisticated than ever about those aspects of politics that they are permitted to understand, which are mostly the superficial ones—who's up, who's down, whom my side hates this week. Forget the acronym POTUS. The public now knows all about talking points, which used to be taboo as a slightly shameful industry secret. Pundits did not want to admit that they cribbed their arguments from an email blast from headquarters, just as presidents used to deny up and down that they consulted pollsters on anything important, until sometime around Carter and Reagan when they started admitting the obvious, that they polled and focus-tested every decision down to the color of their ties.

This peeking behind the curtain has carried the arts of public relations to the maximum point of refinement. As PR professionals get better and better at controlling information, the last remnants of spontaneity and candor have been driven out of the public square. If Aaron Sorkin were researching *Sports Night* today, he would not be allowed to wander around the ESPN mother ship in Bristol unescorted. In every meeting he had, ESPN would have a press officer sitting unobtrusively in the background to make sure none of the employees went off message. If he were researching *The West Wing*, a White House press officer would never leave Sorkin's side.

The common factor behind all these changes, as Sorkin himself could have predicted, is television. But David Sarnoff's great communications medium hasn't made the world better informed; it has just made us feel as if we were. Looking at the consequences of television, from politics to journalism, one starts to wonder whether pseudo-knowledge might be worse than no knowledge at all.

Speaking of pseudo-knowledge, Sarnoff never actually said that quotation about ending misery and ignorance by pointing a camera at them. Philo Farnsworth, the Mormon farm boy whose invention Sarnoff stole, had a famous quotation about television that he *did* actually say: "Television is a gift of God, and God will hold those who utilize his divine instrument accountable to him." From the beginning of his TV career, Sorkin has wanted to be God's avenging angel, holding accountable those who would pervert the world's most powerful medium for inferior purposes. After two decades, the villains he castigated are riding high, and Sorkin has sworn off TV. From now on, he says, he's sticking to movies. Sorkin proved with *The West Wing* that he was right all along about the influence television wields. Who would have thought that a Wednesday night TV drama would change how the people who work in the White House view their own jobs? But if Sorkin ever wants to see the abusers of TV's great power punished, he had better hope that he's wrong about the afterlife and the evangelical Christians he hates so much are right.

4

JEFFREY SACHS

The last chapter of *Eminent Victorians* is about General Charles George Gordon, the man known to history as Gordon of Khartoum. Khartoum was merely the last of many places to which Gordon's name was attached. In three decades of service in the British army he was sent all over the world: to blow up Russian docks in Sevastopol, to negotiate a peace treaty in Basutoland, to evaluate the coastal defenses of Mauritius, to retake Soochow from the Taipings on behalf of the Manchu emperor. The only corner of the empire where he did not serve was India. He did spend one day there as private secretary to the viceroy Lord Ripon in 1880, but he resigned the position upon being asked to write a thank-you note assuring a local dignitary that the viceroy "would read with much pleasure" his gift of a book of Parsi poetry. This diplomatic lie was more than Gordon's conscience could bear, so he paid back his £68 in passage money and took the next mail steamer for Peking, where looming war between China and Russia held out promise of more active employment.

Professor Jeffrey Sachs, formerly of Harvard University and currently Quetelet Professor of Sustainable Development at Columbia, would resent any comparison to the man whose globe-straddling career exemplified the British Empire in high summer. To Sachs, the very word "empire" is a slur. His bestselling book *The End of Poverty* emphatically denies any resemblance to "the infamous 'white man's burden,' the right and obligation of European and European-descended whites to rule the lives of others around the world, which they blithely did with a contradictory mix of naïveté, compassion, and brutality."

Still, it is hard not to notice that Sachs's career as a development economist has been essentially identical to the imperial project. He goes to foreign countries to which he has no previous connection and tells them how to run their governments. It is no use protesting that he was invited. Gordon was invited everywhere he went, too. It was an order from the Chinese emperor that plucked the thirty-year-old Captain Gordon from the Royal Engineers and put him in command of the Ever Victorious Army with the rank of *Tsungping*, equivalent to a brigadier general. As governor-general of Equatoria, Gordon reported directly to the khedive of Egypt, who had the authority to command him and, in 1880, to dismiss him. Gordon became a national hero famous enough for Lytton Strachey to write about after his martyrdom in 1885, when William Gladstone's government left him besieged in Khartoum for 322 days without sending a relief expedition. The reason London left Gordon to die was that his mission was technically under Egyptian auspices and therefore no business of theirs.

Not one of the supposed differences between Sachs and his imperial predecessors amounts to very much, once the usual slanders have been rebutted. The Victorians were intolerant? During the Mahdist rebellion that eventually cost him his head, Gordon re-opened mosques that had been seized for storing gunpowder and wrote in his journal, "The Mussulman worships God as well as I do, and is as acceptable, if sincere, as any Christian." The Victorians resorted too quickly to force? Gordon endured interminable parlays with Sudanese tribal chieftains because "it is better to be tired and wait than that one poor black skin should have a bullet in it." They disregarded the wishes of local people? Even with the Mahdi's guns trained on Khartoum and taking potshots at his bedroom window every night, Gordon avowed, "If I thought the town wished the Mahdi, I would give it up: so much do I respect free will."

Sachs, like most other Americans working in what we have learned diplomatically to call the underdeveloped world, believes that his work is like the nasty old imperialists' but with the bad bits thrown out. The first half of that is true; the second half is almost the opposite of the truth.

Jeffrey Sachs fell into development economics by accident. Nothing about his upbringing in the Detroit suburb of Oak Park, Michigan, had been particularly international. His father, Theodore Sachs, was the state's most famous labor lawyer, so the household atmosphere was liberal, but not in a way that took young Jeff much further afield than an antiwar protest in Ann Arbor or a Cesar Chavez rally in Lansing.

Nor would anyone have expected such a wunderkind to squander his academic reputation on a backwater specialty like development economics. Sachs graduated summa cum laude from Harvard in 1976, received his PhD in 1980 (so quickly because he had already done much of the coursework as an undergraduate), and just three years later was awarded tenure at the astonishing age of twenty-eight. It was the same day that Harvard granted tenure to Larry Summers, a man younger than Sachs by three weeks whose subsequent résumé suggests some of the perches—White House, Treasury, World Bank—that would have been Sachs's if his career had not been sent off in a different direction by a casual invitation from a former student.

David Blanco, the former student, was no raw youth. Eight years older than Sachs, Blanco had come to the Kennedy School in the early 1980s, having already served in Bolivia as finance minister and director of its central bank. He used to joke with Sachs that he was taking his course "to try to understand exactly what he had done while in office." In 1985, he was back at Harvard with a delegation from the Bolivian government looking for advice on how to solve their country's raging hyperinflation, which had hit 20,000 percent the previous year and was on track to hit 60,000 percent the next. Sachs's own academic focus so far had been on First World problems like wage growth and stagflation, but he happened to have a meeting scheduled with the World Bank shortly after and thought that some fresh scoop from Bolivia would add a nice touch to his presentation.

Recounting the story in *The End of Poverty*, Sachs makes no attempt to disguise his youthful arrogance as he listened to the Bolivian delegation describe their country's troubles. "Walking to the blackboard with great confidence, I said, 'Here's how it works.' After I put down the chalk, a voice at the back of the room said, 'Well, if you're so smart, why don't you come to La Paz to help us?' I laughed. And he called out again, 'I mean it.'"

Foreign advisers were nothing new in Bolivia. In the 1960s, the U.S. ambassador Ben Stephansky used to officiate President Víctor Paz Estenssoro's cabinet meetings—as well he might, considering that by 1964 foreign aid from the Alliance for Progress, President John F. Kennedy's "Marshall Plan for Latin America," made up 40 percent of Bolivia's budget. It was American Green Berets who trained the Bolivian commandos who captured and killed Che Guevara in 1967, and Che was a kind of foreign adviser himself, though not a very successful one. Before Bolivia's return to democracy in 1982, several of its dictators had employed the military expertise of one "Lieutenant Colonel Klaus Altmann," actually Klaus Barbie, the Nazi "Butcher of Lyon."

Sachs's advisory style was much more relaxed than Ambassador Stephansky's (and, presumably, Lieutenant Colonel Altmann's). It was endlessly, almost lingeringly deliberative. His main contact in the Bolivian government was Gonzalo Sánchez de Lozada, the planning minister, known to everyone as Goni, who lived in the United States until he was twenty-one and still speaks Spanish with an American accent. Naturally Sachs found him easy to connect with. "Some of these philosophical debates meant weeks and weeks around [Goni's] kitchen table, arguing the philosophical merits of one approach after another," Sachs reminisced later. "From tax reform to trade policy reform, to institutional reform of the government and the judiciary and the state sector, to renegotiating foreign debts, to introducing social policies, to introducing emergency social assistance, and so forth."

These kitchen table bull sessions with Goni came later, after the immediate hyperinflation crisis had been solved. That took three weeks: one to convince the new government that reform was possible, one to debate shock therapy versus gradualism, and one to write up the plan. Even in that initial phase, the reformers were careful not to proceed until everyone in the government had been talked around to agreement. President Paz Estenssoro went into his first cabinet meeting "with Goni's plan in his hand," as Sachs tells the story, and explained to the cabinet members assembled, "Nobody leaves. No one talks to the press. We're going to debate and then agree on an economic strategy. And we're all going to sign it. If you want to resign, you can resign. But otherwise, you're in the government, and you're going to be part of this."

The cabinet might have reached consensus, but the people of Bolivia were simply stuck with Supreme Decree 21060, which devalued the currency, froze government wages, ended price subsidies, opened borders to foreign imports, and allowed for mass layoffs at government-owned mines. More than a hundred labor leaders were detained in a remote Amazonian village for the first ninety days after the reforms were launched as a state of siege was declared and normal rule of law suspended. One can hardly blame the government for resorting to rule by decree in a country that still holds the world record for most coups d'état in history (188 in 150 years), and to their credit, the return to legality was swift and full. It was nonetheless an early example of the way shock therapy would frequently be imposed over popular objections.

Did it work? Yes, insofar as the hyperinflation crisis ended. Inflation dropped from five digits to 9 percent within a year. But Bolivia's standard of living is still among the lowest in South America, closer to Haiti's than to Argentina's. Well into the 1990s, the country still had no paved roads connecting it to any of its five neighbors. The miners who were laid off in 1985 turned to farming coca, setting the stage for U.S. military intervention on and off over the next decade. Sachs's protégé Goni was elected to the presidency in 1993 and 2002, suggesting that the people of Bolivia couldn't have hated his neoliberalism too much, but Goni's successor as president was Evo Morales, a left-wing socialist who in 2013 expelled the U.S. Agency for International Development from the country, putting a decisive end to more than five decades of well-intentioned American meddling. But none of that makes Sachs's mission any less of a success.

Sachs has said that he went to Bolivia because he wanted to witness living history. Hyperinflation was something he had studied in textbooks but never expected to see in his lifetime. At the very moment his new career as "the Indiana Jones of economics" (*The New York Times*) was hitting its peak, with governments all over the world clamoring for his services, history presented Sachs with an even more singular opportunity: the fall of Communism in Eastern Europe. The very month that Solidarity was legalized, in the spring of 1989, Sachs took the first of many trips to Poland in order to advise the victorious dissidents on their unprecedented transition from Communism to capitalism.

It is difficult to grasp just how much the Poles had to learn about the basics of a market economy. Even their accounting system was incompatible with capitalism, data frequently being listed in natural units (for example, jars of jam) instead of money, because planners were more interested in production figures than in profits. Foreigners who bought Polish companies often found that they had to fire everyone in management, because the old managers were embedded in the networks of personal favors and side deals that had been the basis of all business relationships under Communism. State assets had to be sold off, but by whom, for how much, and according to what criteria?

Solidarity had no immediate answers to these questions, because the party was a hodgepodge coalition and its election platform had avoided specifics beyond an end to Soviet tyranny. In the first free elections in 1989, the Communists' feeble slogan had been "Our Faults Are Known." Solidarity's faults were *not* known, and in a sense hardly mattered, but in retrospect it is fair to wonder how many Polish voters would have felt greater trepidation about casting their ballots for Solidarity if they had known what was in store and how bleak things were going to get.

Poland's sweeping economic reform package, called the Balcerowicz Plan after the finance minister, was launched on January 1, 1990. Overnight, state-owned enterprises lost their privileges, the złoty became internationally convertible, foreign investment was permitted, price controls were mostly abolished—and Poland's reward was to see its GDP shrink 11.6 percent that year. Poland moved faster than any post-Communist country to pass a framework of corporate law to allow entrepreneurs to start private enterprises, and by the end of 1991 hundreds of thousands of companies had been registered. That year GDP shrank a further 7.3 percent. Poland returned to growth in 1992, but even two years after it turned that corner, unemployment was still above 16 percent and the symbolically important Gdańsk Shipyard had been shut down as unprofitable.

Things were not quite as bad as the figures suggested. The supposed decline in living standards was measured against the artificially low prices and high wages of terminal Communism and took no account of the prices people had actually been paying on the black market, when the items they wanted were available at all. The 600 percent inflation that gave everyone a scare in the early months of 1990 was quickly tamed. Surveys showed that 64 percent of Poles thought corruption was worse under capitalism than Communism, but that perception was fueled by rampant rumors and conspiracy theories (for example, that American competitors were using the privatization process to steal Polish trade secrets), very few of which were true. When the governor of Silesia set up a corruption hotline in response to these rumors, investigators were able to confirm only six cases out of a thousand.

Regardless of whether the public's perception of shock therapy was accurate, it remained unpopular. Politicians ever since have been eager to distance themselves from it—and from Sachs. "Professor Jeffrey Sachs of Harvard is not an economic adviser to the Polish Government," read an official statement issued by the president's press office to the *Financial Times* in 1991. "Professor Sachs visits Poland often and his visits are welcome but he has no official role with the government." The man who first approached Sachs about consulting for Solidarity, Krzysztof Krowacki of the Washington embassy, expressed his doubts to a reporter within a few months: "Sometimes I get the idea that people think he has a contract with the government of Poland, which he doesn't." Even Leszek Balcerowicz, who has been a steadfast defender of his namesake plan, bristled when an American interviewer asked him whether Poland had "adopted the Sachs program." He reminded him, "We worked on the Polish program in Poland for 12 years."

These repudiations were at least a little disingenuous. Let it be granted that Sachs is a gifted self-promoter and that the much-hyped "shock therapy" brand obscured the fact that his advice was little different from what the International Monetary Fund was saying. Nevertheless, there was at least one occasion when Sachs changed the trajectory of market reform in Poland single-handedly. Other Western consultants gave their advice to Solidarity behind closed doors. Sachs did plenty of that, but he also gave a speech to the Solidarity parliamentary caucus in September 1989 that was broadcast on national television. From a podium in the Sejm, he offered a stirring call for bold action. Figure out how fast you can move, he said, and then move three times faster. "He talked in such a smooth, confident manner that many responded as if they were hearing a revelation," one MP later said. Sachs sold the reforms to the public in a way that cold-fish Balcerowicz or economically illiterate Lech Wałesa could never have done.

Still, these politically convenient disavowals of Sachs were technically true. He *hadn't* been employed by the Polish government. His initial trips were paid for by George Soros, his later ones by the United Nations University in Helsinki. That was the most remarkable thing about the foreign advisers who descended on Poland in the early 1990s: how few of them were directly employed by the Poles. Two-thirds of the money USAID spent in Eastern Europe in 1991 went to "technical assistance," which meant it was hoovered up by contractors like the Big Six accounting firms for their fees and expenses. The Polish vice-minister of finance complained of these advisers that "the U.S. government is paying them to provide advice to us without asking us, even without informing us." Sardonic officials joked that USAID seemed to be solving the West's unemployment problem, not Poland's.

The Western advisers who offered their services to the Wałesa government genuinely wanted to help the Polish people. Sachs himself said that Solidarity "were political heroes of mine," and no one can doubt his sincerity. But those brave heroes did not sign his paychecks. Sachs and his fellow ambassadors from the free world were advising a government they did not ultimately answer to, which made their labors fundamentally imperial.

When Jeffrey Sachs departed Poland and left behind, as he thought, a job well done, he did what every great man does when he is overwhelmed by hubris. He decided to go to Russia.

Interviewers say that when asked about his time in Russia, Sachs becomes "defensive," "bristling," "his baritone voice jumping an octave." His biographer, Nina Munk, found that subject made him suddenly "prickly like a hedgehog." A 2001 profile in *The Boston Globe* claimed, "The place still haunts him like a ghost." Allowing for some journalistic license on the *Globe* reporter's part, a certain sensitivity can be detected in Sachs's reply to Munk. "Do I consider Russia a failure of the West? Yes, definitely. Do I consider it a personal failure? No! I find that absolutely preposterous!"

There was certainly enough to feel guilty about. In Bolivia and Poland, the costs of shock therapy had generally fallen into the category of creative destruction. Miners lost their jobs, pensioners lost their savings, but some adjustment was unavoidable, and social programs cushioned the blow. (Sachs made sure of it; no austere Chicago man he.) But in Russia, things were so much worse than they had to be. In the first half of the 1990s, deaths by suicide had doubled, and deaths from alcohol abuse tripled. Between 1989 and 1999, Russia's GDP had dropped *by half.* An economic collapse of that magnitude is not a correction. It is a catastrophe.

Sachs insists that the worst outcomes in Russia were all caused by decisions contrary to his advice. This is quite true. He told the Yeltsin government not to privatize their resource companies right away but rather to keep them in state hands to give the government a stable source of revenue. Instead, they quickly auctioned off Russia's oil and gas assets, which spawned a pernicious class of oligarchs and also worsened the revenue crisis of the late 1990s, when the state proved too weak to collect more than a fraction of the taxes it was owed. Sachs offers many such examples "where my direct advice went unheeded" in a long essay published on his personal website in 2012, "What I Did in Russia," the tone of which suggests that the reporters are right who say Sachs is defensive on the Russia subject.

But it wasn't as an adviser that Sachs inflicted the greatest damage. It was as head of the Harvard Institute for International Development. HIID had been founded in 1962, as the Development Advisory Service (renamed in 1974), for the purpose of sending Harvard economists to places like Colombia, Namibia, and Indonesia to give policy advice. In exchange the economists were allowed to write research papers about their pet programs' results. These projects were frequently underwritten by the United Nations or the Ford Foundation or, in the case of Russia, USAID. Russia was by far the biggest project that HIID had ever undertaken, and it was launched the year Sachs became head of the institute in 1995. In addition to receiving $40 million from USAID directly, HIID oversaw the disbursement of more than $300 million in USAID contracts to other organizations.

The head of HIID's Russia project was Andrei Shleifer, a protégé of Larry Summers's and like Summers both ambitious and precocious; he was only thirty-one when the project launched. Shleifer was Russian-born and emigrated at the relatively late age of fifteen, so he was well placed to connect with the Russians HIID was advising. He cultivated these relationships assiduously—for his own reasons as much as Harvard's, as soon became clear—and they repaid his attentions with loyalty. When USAID awarded one securities-related technical assistance project to Stanford, the Russians whom the project was intended to assist responded that they did not want Stanford's help. A fresh contract for the same project was then drawn up and given to the Russians' preferred choice: Harvard.

Most Russians were resentful of the foreign advisers who descended on their country at the moment of its greatest humiliation, and this resentment only grew worse as the West's army of consultants, experts, and NGO workers fanned out into the provinces where ordinary Russians could see them with their own eyes. The BBC journalist Angus Roxburgh witnessed a very tense land auction outside Nizhny Novgorod in 1992 where "a young man and woman, straight from Harvard," presided over the dismemberment of what had been, until recently, collective farms. Sachs himself was known to engage in Ugly American behavior, like putting his feet up in the waiting room of Minister of Finance Yegor Gaidar until the minister's secretary came over and asked him, in front of a roomful of patiently waiting officials, "Excuse me, Mr. Sachs, would you please take your feet off my table?"

Imagine ordinary Russians' fury, then, when they learned that the Harvard advisers in Moscow were not only arrogant and insensitive but actually corrupt. Shleifer and his hedge fund manager wife turned out to be investing in Russian companies whose fortunes Shleifer was in a position to determine and using insider information from his various advisory posts. Years of no-bid contracts and deference from Washington had allowed this conflict of interest to metastasize, and it was only a General Accounting Office audit that alerted USAID to the problem. A federal investigation was launched, which ended with Harvard's agreeing to pay the largest settlement in the university's history, $26.5 million. Shleifer personally settled with the U.S. government for $2 million and had to mortgage his house. He managed to keep his faculty position at Harvard, thanks to Larry Summers, who became president of the university in 2001.

When the scandal erupted in 1999, Sachs resigned as head of HIID, though no one ever alleged that he himself did anything corrupt. Indeed, he had every right to protest that he acted as soon as he became aware of any impropriety and that he wasn't even in Russia at the time of Shleifer's misdeeds; he hasn't been back there since 1995. Privately he might add that the people who made his resignation necessary were old rivals who might well have relished having made him look bad. Summers and Shleifer were always much more worldly than Sachs, and his idealism seemed to rub them the wrong way.

But the scandal *was* Sachs's responsibility, not because he was technically Shleifer's boss, but because Shleifer was only in Russia at all because of the trail Sachs had blazed. Advising foreign governments in this way was a career path he practically invented. Even as late as his stint in Poland, Sachs observed with chagrin that his academic colleagues were baffled by what he was doing. "Communism was falling, and I was pinching myself, because I was in the center of this, absolutely the epicenter of it, saying, 'Where *is* everybody?'" It wasn't until Russia that the cynics figured out that all this far-flung do-goodism might have an angle in it.

Ironically, for Sachs foreign advising had been a sacrifice. A *New York Times* profile from 1991 records his Harvard colleagues shaking their heads that poor Jeff Sachs will never win the John Bates Clark Medal now, not unless he gives up globe-trotting and gets back to publishing. "He was clearly capable of doing pretty important work," sighed Robert Barro, "but I don't think he did it." Sachs ignored these ivory-tower critics and followed his own path, out of a combination of self-will and genuine idealism. That idealism ended up creating opportunities for canny operators like Shleifer to rob the very people Sachs was trying to help.

Sachs never did win the John Bates Clark Medal. Shleifer did, in 1999.

Investment bankers who specialize in emerging markets have a saying: "In Russia, if you make them mad, they'll kill you. In Africa, if you make them mad, they'll *try* to kill you, but by the time their plan comes together you'll be gone." By the time Sachs disentangled himself from Russia, everyone there wanted to kill him, but he was already gone—to Africa.

Ten years passed between Sachs's first trip to Bolivia in 1985 and the last time he set foot in Russia in 1995, which was also, incidentally, the year he saw Africa for the first time. Like his earlier rise from novice consultant to celebrity "Dr. Shock," Sachs's rise to preeminence in the field of humanitarian aid unfolded rapidly. It was exactly ten years again between his first trip to Zambia and the banner year when Sachs released his bestselling book *The End of Poverty* and launched the first Millennium Villages project, in a bid to revolutionize the way the developed world fights extreme poverty.

When HIID was dissolved after the Shleifer scandal, Sachs stayed on for a while at the renamed Center for International Development but was clearly casting around for a new project. He found one when the director of the World Health Organization invited him to lead its newly launched Commission on Macroeconomics and Health. For two years he supervised more than a hundred experts in a dozen different fields to produce a two-hundred-page final report on the diseases of poverty.

Sachs used this time to get his bearings in the aid world. These humanitarians and philanthropists were a different set from the finance ministers and budget wonks he had previously worked with, and Sachs took a few years to work out what his distinctive contribution to this new field might be. Paul Farmer, a Harvard-trained physician known for his work in Haiti, remembers Sachs visiting his clinic there in 2001. "Jeff really changed the way we think about the problem of health," he told Sachs's biographer. " 'You guys'— meaning, you people in medicine and public health—'you have to stop using the M-word and start using the B-word.' In other words, you don't need millions of dollars to fix this, you need billions of dollars."

Sachs himself had no trouble thinking big. In 2002, he accepted two offers: one from the UN secretary-general, Kofi Annan, to be his personal adviser on the Millennium Development Goals, and another from Columbia University to head up its Earth Institute, an academic empire with eight hundred employees and an annual budget of $87 million. He had learned from his apprenticeship at the WHO that there was an opening in the field of humanitarian aid for someone with his prodigious powers of self-promotion. He had also learned that donors were susceptible to requests framed in economist's terms like "return on investment." His blockbuster WHO report, for example, had claimed that $66 billion in AIDS and malaria spending would yield $360 billion in economic growth. With those lessons in hand, Sachs was ready to launch his signature program, the Millennium Villages project.

The Millennium Villages project is a strangely postmodern enterprise. Officially, it does the same thing every development program does: gives impoverished villages fertilizer, high-yield seeds, solar panels, school lunches, a new well. But the year Sachs spent traveling with Bono on the rock star's Jubilee 2000 debt forgiveness tour was not wasted. He learned the power of celebrity. He introduced his project to the wider world with the MTV documentary *The Diary of Angelina Jolie and Dr. Jeffrey Sachs in Africa*. He campaigned for donations with Hollywood stars like Sharon Stone, Richard Gere, and Madonna, who gave $1.5 million of her own money, some of it earmarked to build a school in Malawi that would teach, among other classes, Kabbalah spirituality. Other aid projects claim to alleviate poverty. Sachs claimed that the Millennium Villages model would quite literally *end* extreme poverty within the present generation, once it perfected its methods for enabling poor Africans to "get their foot on the ladder of development" and was scaled up from fourteen villages to the rest of the continent.

Was Sachs "on a quest for some kind of redemption, after his failure in Russia?" as one journalist phrased it, echoing a popular theory. Sachs insists not: "I am the same person I always was." Whether or not he is motivated by guilt, there is no doubt that he has learned lessons from his experience in Russia. There, he was blamed for things that weren't his fault. Now he operates on the assumption that if you're going to be blamed whether the politicians listen to you or not, you had better make sure they listen to you. That, at least, would explain his newfound tendency to bellow, insult, and abuse people who stand in the way of his objectives. "He's a bully," says one deputy secretary-general who worked with Sachs at the United Nations. "For the record, he's a bully."

Sachs did not start out as a bully by disposition. It was a trait he acquired. As late as 1997, when he got into a brief spat with Summers (again) and the IMF over the Asian financial crisis, he allowed himself to be cowed at a private conference in Boston when the economists he had been criticizing in the press confronted him over the hypocrisy of his being conciliatory in private but vituperative in public. He attempted to defend his public remarks as within the bounds of fair debate, when Stanley Fischer—famously the most mild-mannered fellow at the IMF—interrupted him to shout, "You know that's not true!" and "tick off five occasions in which Sachs had publicly impugned his competence and integrity," according to *The Washington Post.*

If Sachs was bashful about insulting people then, he isn't now. His mass emails are known to include incandescent lines like "Frankly, I find your approach disreputable as well as economically ignorant." On the phone, he can be overheard shouting things like "He's a punk! He can go to hell!" When a questioner at one of his lectures asked whether his proposal to give away antimalarial bed nets might not undermine African sellers who had built up a market for them, he responded not with reasoned argument but by shouting, "Children are dying, for God's sake!" His reputation for bullying doesn't seem to bother him, perhaps because these tantrums are tactical. "I advise Africa's governments to come right out and demand money from the donor agencies—and then demand it again. And again. That's what I do. I write a letter. Then another letter. Then an op-ed. And then I throw a tantrum. In the end, the money may appear—if only so they can get rid of me."

Yet he is probably more of a jerk than he needs to be. Nina Munk witnessed one eruption that brought Sachs no obvious tactical advantage but only made the other business class passengers on the flight to Dar es Salaam feel uncomfortable. "These deaths are on your hands!" Sachs shouted at a Swiss malaria expert who had criticized Sachs's proposed mass giveaway of bed nets. "You do not know the facts," the man replied calmly. "What I know is you're letting people die!" "I do not need to be insulted," the man said, walking away. Sachs shouted after him, "Your actions are reprehensible! I hope you know that!"

One side effect of this tempestuousness is that his peers have become extremely reluctant to criticize him. Those who dare to do so inevitably find one of Sachs's famous poison-pen emails in their in-boxes. "I was really shaken up," admitted one recipient, a professor at Berkeley, to a reporter from *Foreign Policy* magazine. "We're all so puzzled by the kind of hysterical attacks on anybody who criticizes Millennium Villages." The only safe way to criticize Sachs is from a solid foundation of facts, and this is difficult when the Millennium Villages project keeps a tight hold on its data through nondisclosure agreements. One peer-reviewed *Lancet* paper that Sachs co-authored, claiming that malaria deaths among children had dropped three times faster in Millennium Villages than outside them, had to be retracted when sharp-eyed researchers spotted a flaw in their calculations. But such direct hits are rare, especially because Sachs long refused to have control villages to measure the project's achievements against—on moral grounds, because it would be wrong to have villages that he deliberately didn't help.

For a long time, Sachs's most prominent critic was William Easterly, a maverick development economist and World Bank veteran who also knew Africa of old, having lived in Ghana for a year when he was twelve when his father was a professor of biology there. The thrust of Easterly's critique is Hayekian. Planners don't know what needs are most important to the desperately poor, or what economic activities might bring them a profit on the open market after the planner's subsidies have expired, so they should invest in these communities rather than subsidize them and let poor Africans' own initiative, in combination with the free market, determine where scarce dollars should go. Within development economics, the feud between Sachs and Easterly has come to represent competing schools of thought: top-down versus bottom-up, global solutions versus local initiative, big pushes versus incremental improvements.

This dichotomy was always essentially fruitless. Every aid program is some combination of top-down and bottom-up. Even the

Millennium Villages project claims that it is as bottom-up as is feasible. It does, after all, consult extensively with its villagers to determine what amenities they want (or are willing to tell aid workers they want, not always the same thing). Some problems are best solved by simply giving aid recipients what they ask for—but not all. What about villagers who persist in breeding more cattle than their land can bear, even though it makes their herds thinner and sicker, because they measure wealth in cattle counted by the head? If you leave the very poor to their own devices completely, they will only persist in the behaviors that made them poor in the first place.

There is no magic formula for economic development. Not "sustainability," not "accountability," not any of the development catchphrases of yesteryear. Who now puts their faith in "turnpikes," "golden rules," or "I/O-based planning"? There is only imperfect human judgment, and there is no substitute for learning from experience. Sachs and Easterly are therefore equally wrong, insofar as both of them have cut themselves off from the greatest fund of experience available to them—the great liberal empires. Easterly has condemned the old empires as "paternalistic," "coercive," and "racist." Sachs's view of empire we know. Alas, those old Victorians have abundant lessons to teach today's development experts, if they could only own up to the resemblance. But no American, and certainly no boomer, could possibly do that.

The United States' crusade against empire was our most important contribution to twentieth-century geopolitics. Far more consequential than the defeat of the upstart Soviet Empire in 1989 was our dismantling of the older, richer, bigger European empires after

World War II. Poor Britain and France, they thought they had *won* the war. They were accustomed to hearing Americans natter on about self-determination ever since their brush with Woodrow Wilson. They did not realize that when Franklin Roosevelt said, "America won't help England in this war simply so that she will be able to continue to ride roughshod over colonial peoples," he meant it. The Universal Declaration of Human Rights in 1948 included the right to a "nationality" in there with life, liberty, and security of person, and over the next three decades the United States saw to it that this brand-new right was enforced.

Both sides of American politics, Republicans and Democrats, believed that America was well positioned to befriend Third World nationalist movements, as an anticolonial nation itself. John Foster Dulles told a visiting European diplomat that Arab nationalism, for example, was "a turbulent stream" but "the United States did not have the slightest intention of trying to stem it." Instead, they would "erect dikes to contain it," and "later on, when the turbulence of the stream has moderated, we would hope to work with it." The British and French could hardly believe our naïveté. They knew a different riparian metaphor for revolution, the Persian verse quoted by Michael O'Dwyer in his memoir *India as I Knew It* (1925) to describe his experience with unrest as lieutenant governor of the Punjab:

Sar-i-Chashna ba bayad giriftan bá mil,
Chi pur shud na shayad guzashtan ba fil.

A stream can be stopped at its source by a twig,
Let it flow, and it will drown even an elephant.

O'Dwyer's love of Eastern literature earned him no credit with the Indian nationalists, one of whom assassinated him in London in 1940.

Dulles's and Eisenhower's credulousness about Arab nationalism led them to intervene on Nasser's behalf during the Suez Crisis, the watershed moment in decolonization after which the fall of the remaining imperial holdouts was a technicality. Suez was typical of anticolonial wars in that Nasser lost militarily but was handed victory on a platter by his more powerful allies. The British prime minister, Anthony Eden, had no choice but to capitulate to Eisenhower's demands, because American loans were propping up his country and his currency. The supposed loss of imperial nerve that everyone blames for the fall of the British Empire was not spontaneous. It arose only after Britain realized that America was not just willing but very happy to see Nasser seize the Suez Canal in violation of all international law and assume leadership of an anti-imperial groundswell across the Middle East. The United States even gave Nasser radio equipment and propaganda training to help him broadcast his message to the Arab street. Again and again, on almost every continent, America signaled its support for nationalists against imperialists—aiding African guerrillas, drafting anti-French propaganda flyers in Vietnam. If the colonial powers resisted, America's economic leverage gave them the last word, but by the late 1960s what little resistance there was had been worn down.

Around that time, it was beginning to become clear that endorsing anticolonial nationalism had been a mistake. For one thing, it spawned the cold war. Without decolonization there would not have been a slew of young and unstable nations for the superpowers to fight over. America itself gained no benefit from its anti-imperial stance, for the nationalists (Nasser included) continued their anti-American rhetoric as before. Anyone who wished to consider the question from the oppressed peoples' point of view had to conclude that, by any objective criteria, they were no better off. Their new leaders were tyrants and demagogues; they no longer enjoyed the protection of the rule of law; and their economies, which had experienced the postwar boom along with everyone else (exports from British Africa increased by a factor of five between 1947 and 1960), suddenly tanked. Ghana was chosen to be the first African colony that the British let go because its thriving cocoa industry was thought to give it a sound economic base. After two decades of calamitous mismanagement, Ghana's cocoa production had declined by half.

But every time the flaws of doctrinaire anti-imperialism became clear, another generation came onto the scene and embraced the crusade with new fervor, and none with more fervor than the boomers. A curious lexicographical fact: while "empire" is an ancient term, "imperialism" arose only in the late nineteenth century and "colonialism" is pure 1960s vintage. As everyone knows, the fastest way to discredit something is to make it an "-ism." Empire is the oldest and most common type of polity in world history, but it took only a few generations of idealistic Americans to declare it comprehensively prohibited for all time.

Of course, America still had a superpower's responsibilities to take care of. For this we invented a new kind of non-empire, an empire without the bad stuff—a virginal imperialism. Initially, this took the form of "Marshall Plans" for everything. The first of these was directed at Latin America, the Alliance for Progress, or Alianza para el Progreso. Actually, the speechwriter Richard Goodwin originally christened it the "Alianza para Progreso," which is grammatically incorrect, as President Kennedy was embarrassed to discover after he used Goodwin's phrase in his early speeches on the subject. This would not be the last time American aid was undermined by displays of ignorance. In the end the Alliance for Progress failed to achieve the objectives laid out in its charter, though not for lack of funds: America spent billions more on it than on the Marshall Plan itself. The causes of Latin American poverty were simply more entrenched than the Kennedy team thought.

America's "Marshall Plan for Africa" never called itself that, though it cost just as much. Instead, it was called "foreign aid" and "development assistance"—Jeffrey Sachs's world. Of course, by the time Sachs came along, development had already reached the point of decadence. Over a span of fifty years, America went from sending Africa brigades of engineers to sending brigades of economists, who did not even know how to build anything. By the 1990s we were sending PR consultants, who did not even *know* anything. Today the most sought-after Africa hands are people like Jeffrey Smith, executive director of a nonprofit PR firm who is most famous for engineering the overthrow of the dictator of Gambia from his Twitter account.

After nearly a century of America's virginal imperialism, it seems evident that all of the contortions we undergo to make our global hegemony less imperial only make us less effective and frequently make us look absurd. Laundering our imperialism through international organizations like the UN means entrusting our missions to people from Third World countries themselves who often do everything they can to prolong their postings because, as one aid veteran told the journalist David Rieff, "these guys have only one idea, it's I don't want to have to go back to Dhaka or wherever." Other proxies are worse. In our effective protectorate of Kosovo, our handpicked president was head of the Kosovo Liberation Army at a time when it was murdering Serbs and selling their organs on the black market. The British preferred to rule through local chieftains when possible, but they would have balked at that.

The post–cold war period also saw the United States replace meddlesome CIA operatives with no less meddlesome NGO workers. These NGOs are "nongovernmental" only in the technical sense. Groups like Freedom House and the National Endowment for Democracy receive more than 80 percent of their funds from congressional appropriations. Whether they realize it or not, these NGO workers are the heirs not only of the CIA but of the old colonialists. The humanitarian ones are like district commissioners, out in the field teaching agricultural techniques, distributing seeds, vaccinating children, mediating local conflicts. Others are like high commissioners, working with the politicians who nominally govern these countries, instructing them in the proper way to run their parliaments, their armies, their political parties. The only difference is that if our wards become intransigent, we cannot, in the last resort, simply tell them what to do. Instead, we must replace them with the reformers-in-waiting our other NGOs have been training with their "civil society building" programs. A lot of trouble to go to, just so that we can exercise imperial power without admitting to it.

George Santayana's second most famous quotation, after the one about history repeating, is the one about the British Empire: "Never since the heroic days of Greece has the world had such a sweet, just, boyish master." No one ever quotes the line that follows, which, in more ways than Santayana could have intended, refers to us: "It will be a black day for the human race when scientific blackguards, conspirators, churls, and fanatics manage to supplant him."

Now Jeffrey Sachs has come home. "When I started my career," he told the Oxford Union in 2017, "I said to myself, I don't really have to work on the United States, because we're rich. . . . Starting in the early 2000s, I started feeling that not only is the United States not a role model but it's really messed up." Three of his last four books have been about American politics, one carrying a foreword by Senator Bernie Sanders. In 2011, Sachs wandered downtown from the Upper West Side town house that Columbia gave him along with his salary to entice him away from Harvard and joined the Occupy Wall Street protesters in Zuccotti Park. News cameras captured his impassioned indictment of Wall Street greed and his endorsement of the young activists attempting to make the rich pay their fair share.

Object to his endorsement of Occupy Wall Street if you must, but don't call it hypocrisy. Occupy was *exactly* the sort of rebel movement that the United States would pour money into if this were a foreign country. They were not very practical-minded, but America's designated reformers don't have to be. They can be poets. Technocrats will be on hand to take care of the rest. As Lord Derby reassured Benjamin Disraeli when the unmathematical Dizzy hesitated to accept Derby's offer to be his Chancellor of the Exchequer, "Don't worry, they give you the figures." Whether it's the dissident intellectuals of the Color Revolutions or the African presidents with degrees in business administration from SUNY Buffalo, the advisees of America's empire don't have to know much. They only have to know to call someone like Jeffrey Sachs.

People who knew him in his "shock therapy" days have accused Sachs of an ideological reversal. One Polish politician has sneered in his memoirs, "There are times now that he appears to be closer to St. Francis than to Balcerowicz." These critics say there is a massive inconsistency in acting as the apostle of neoliberalism one day and getting Bernie Sanders to write the foreword to your book the next. Sachs, however, insists he hasn't changed. And he's right.

5

CAMILLE PAGLIA

Nothing about Camille Paglia is old-fashioned, except her job description. The scholar-celebrity is not a type much seen anymore. Gone are the days when Columbia University professors like Mark Van Doren and Jacques Barzun were sought after on TV and radio. The boomers' favorite celebrities were more likely to be rock stars and Hollywood actors. But since her launch into fame in the early 1990s, Paglia has brought rock star panache to academic debate in a way like no one else.

This did not always sit well with her more buttoned-up predecessors. Susan Sontag, the glamorous scholar-celebrity the young Paglia most resembled, was born in 1933 and came up among New York's early cold war intellectuals, and by her old-fashioned standards Paglia was much too manic and brash, even in her essays on literary subjects, to say nothing of her splashy op-eds on date rape and political correctness. Sontag perhaps did not realize that when she advertised the tension between them, she was only juicing the younger woman's career. The feud that developed suited Paglia's boomer persona to perfection: half highbrow rivalry, half tabloid catfight, with an underlying theme of the old guard being overthrown by young rebels.

The feud began decades before Sontag was even aware of it. The two women first met in 1973 when Sontag was a world-famous intellectual and Paglia merely an obscure Bennington professor who had invited her to campus to give a lecture. The night ended up going very badly and ruining Paglia's credibility at Bennington as an inviter of guest speakers. After arriving two hours late, Sontag failed to deliver a lecture on the cultural scene, as promised, but instead read a new short story, which Paglia found "vapid" and the crowd found interminable. Sontag then proceeded to act the diva at the reception in her honor, and Paglia was left feeling that she had lost a hero and gained a grievance worth avenging. Even then, Paglia remembers, she wanted to shout at Sontag, "I'm your successor, dammit, and you don't have the wit to realize it!"

Twenty years later, when her first book came out, Paglia stoked this resentment into a full-blown rivalry by giving provocative quotations to *Vanity Fair* and the *New York Post*'s Page Six ("I've been chasing that bitch for 25 years and I've finally passed her"). Sontag was goaded into responding, sullenly, not only by Paglia's sniping but also by frequent questioning from interviewers about whether she thought this new writer named Camille Paglia ought to be considered her successor.

At stake in this feud was which of these two women would be the preeminent female public intellectual of the 1990s. Paglia would win that contest. But first she had to build herself into a credible challenger. The years between 1973 and 1990 would be difficult ones, full of professional rejection, financial hardship, and monastic isolation, but in the end Paglia became the contender she always thought she could be, by force of will and by the power of her intellect.

She would begin by establishing her expertise in a subject that Sontag had claimed for her own in the *Partisan Review* essay that had launched her career, "Notes on 'Camp' ": the perverse, epicene, theatrical school of the nineteenth-century decadents.

The literary movement known as decadence arose in France in 1884, at a time when the nation appeared to be on its deathbed, if not already advanced into putrefaction. Authors like Joris-Karl Huysmans looked at France and saw in it an ancient aristocratic house, going all the way back to Rome, whose last scion was too feckless to produce an heir or do much of anything except luxuriate in the vices of the Belle Epoque. This pessimism was not just an affectation of the bohemian class. Birthrates in France were the lowest in Europe and still falling, and the day when France would be, incredibly, less populous than England was being hastened along by such self-inflicted epidemics as alcoholism and syphilis. No help for these ills could be expected from the governments of the Third Republic, which had proved a double disappointment. The last time France had failed to make a success of democracy, it had at least produced an emperor fit to rank with Caesar and Alexander. Now it produced only corrupt, no-name ministries of insect duration. This was not just a matter of having gotten a bad knock at Sedan. It was, as Flaubert put it in a letter to a friend, "the end of the Latin world."

None of this pessimism survived the trip across the channel when decadence became the vogue in London in the 1890s. "Decadent" to the Victorians, like "sinful" to us, was a chocolate word, connoting nothing worse than indulgence carried to the point of naughtiness. Oscar Wilde adopted it as a brand, as if he were a bar of soap. Arthur Symons adopted it to give a frisson to such otherwise squalid pastimes as getting drunk and sleeping with chorus girls. The only English decadent who took the term seriously was the Oxford don Walter Pater, and for him it merely meant that he had given himself permission to treat English like a dead language. Protestant England did not have France's sense of continuity with Latin civilization, so its decadents did not feel that by flouncing around London spinning paradoxes, they were letting their ancestors down. They were merely enjoying the dividends of a well-run and prosperous empire.

Camille Paglia is a decadent of the Anglo type—which, after all, is the kind anyone would choose to be if they had a choice. They were the nice ones. They were optimists. They were elitists, but they believed in democracy. They even believed in political progress, oddly enough. The poet Algernon Swinburne might have thought the world was a purple orgy of pain and flagellation, but he wrote impassioned republican broadsides against the House of Lords and dedicated a volume of his poetry to Mazzini. (Contrast the French decadent Huysmans: "Democracy is like iodide that draws out the boils of human stupidity.") Very few of the French decadents bothered to have children. In England, even the homosexual ones like Oscar did.

The English called the 1890s the Mauve Decade, and Camille Paglia's is a mauve decadence: corrupt but nonthreatening. "I follow the Decadents in trying to drive Rousseauist benevolence out of discourse on art and nature," she proclaims in *Sexual Personae*—a book that even has the word "decadence" in its subtitle ("Art and Decadence from Nefertiti to Emily Dickinson"). She makes decadence sound dangerous but in a sexy way, a gilded mask held over a knowing smile. Her decadents do not lament the Dionysiac forces straining at the limits of an enfeebled civilization. They savor them, as fervidly as possible. "Decadents satirized the liberal faith in progress with sizzling prophecies of catastrophe," she writes. Sizzling— like a steak, like Paris.

But is it really so much better to be a cheerful decadent? The English movement failed as conclusively as its French counterpart and, if anything, more tragically, insofar as their naïveté was their undoing. Pater withdrew the last chapter of his *Studies in the History of the Renaissance* from the second edition when he observed with dismay that readers were following the Epicurean advice in it ("To burn always with this hard, gemlike flame, to maintain this ecstasy, is success in life") not through aesthetic self-cultivation but with absinthe and sodomy. No decadent—no writer in history— was ever sunk by his own levity more dramatically than Oscar Wilde. No one else would have sparred so flippantly with the prosecuting barrister: "Did you ever kiss him?" "Oh, no, never in my life, he was a peculiarly plain boy."

Wilde's case is worth pausing over, because the version that has gone down in history is wrong, and in a way that covers up the pitfalls of treating decadence frivolously. Today Wilde is remembered as the first gay rights martyr, a victim of Victorian hypocrisy, but that is not how he saw himself. In his letters written after his release from prison, there is no trace of indignation at the philistines who scorned the love that dare not speak its name. His well-deserved downfall, as he came to see it, was self-inflicted, the entirely justified consequence of having allowed himself to become ensnared by a shallow and self-absorbed monster like Lord Alfred Douglas. When friends wrote to him in exile to offer their sympathies, he wrote back that being in prison had made him a better man by teaching him how to suffer. "I accept everything. I am sure it is all right. I was living a life unworthy of an artist." The injustice of the charge against him did not enter into it.

"When in doubt, I read Oscar Wilde," Camille Paglia writes in the introduction to her first essay collection. "His battles are my battles, and there are echoes of his strategies and formulations throughout my work." She wrote truer than she knew, for she has reenacted not only his battles but also his tragedy. Like Wilde, Paglia has dabbled in decadence as if it were a game. The pithy paradoxes, the valorization of glamour, the celebration of sexual daring, have to her been a way of striking a pose, a way to annoy all the academic frumps and feminist scolds who considered Madonna's *Sex* book beneath their attention. Paglia's tragedy, like that of her fin de siècle forebears, is that she toyed with forces that were much more dangerous than she imagined them to be, and they turned on her in the end.

Paglia might have been forgiven for assuming, when she launched on her public career, that her Wildean penance was already behind her. She had certainly paid a price for the extravagant conduct of her youth. She arrived at Yale for graduate school in 1968, after a dazzling undergraduate career at SUNY Binghamton, and even in those heady days she could not find anyone in the English department interested in advising a PhD thesis with so much transvestism and sadomasochism in it. The great critic Harold Bloom eventually rescued her by calling her into his office and saying, "My dear, I am the *only* one who can direct that dissertation." He had never taught her before, but he knew her by reputation. Bloom saved her a second time in May of her graduation year, when she had received no job offers. "Everyone else had been hired six months before," she remembered. "Bennington had a last-minute opening and called up [Bloom] and asked him if anyone interesting was left. He said, yes, there is this rather flamboyant person named Camille Paglia."

On his recommendation she proceeded in 1972 to Bennington College, where she taught an elective called "Aestheticism and Decadence," among other classes. Her Carnaby Street wardrobe and her fascination with the seamy side of the canon made trouble for Paglia there, too. Students began to whisper that Paglia was into witchcraft, that she had made a male student's plane crash because she had a crush on his girlfriend. Six years of confrontational behavior culminated in a fistfight at a school dance. As Paglia told the lesbian magazine *Girlfriends* twenty years later, she had commented to a male advisee that a certain female friend of his seemed to be attracted to her (Paglia's) girlfriend, Patty, an undergraduate. The girl learned of Paglia's remark and, at the dance, "came out of nowhere, went ballistic, and attacked me." Charges against the student were brought, then dropped. Bennington put Paglia on research leave, bought out her contract, and allowed her to quietly resign.

Six years were to pass, six austere years, before Paglia found another full-time academic position. She spent a year at Wesleyan, a year back at Yale, part-time. Nothing worked out. She taught night classes at an aircraft plant. She went deeply into debt. This was hard on the girl who had received only one B in four years at SUNY

Binghamton. All the while, her opus, an expanded version of her Yale dissertation, was rejected by publisher after publisher. Eventually she saw an advertisement for a faculty opening at the Philadelphia College of Performing Arts, threw in an application, and got the job. Reflecting back on this period, Paglia told an interviewer that those hard years of solitary labor granted her the same three things that being Irish gave Stephen Dedalus: "silence, exile, and cunning."

She watched less talented academics mount benignly up the career ladder and assiduously stored up resentments, to which she would give vent when fame finally arrived. Martha Nussbaum, born the same year as Paglia, was all right as long as she stuck to classics, but her underinformed ventures into sexology were for Paglia painful to watch. Elaine Showalter had the nerve to build a career on the Victorian fin de siècle, to the point of publishing a book titled *Daughters of Decadence*, despite herself being straight, a housewife, and a frump. (Showalter would later pan *Sexual Personae*, calling it, bafflingly, "Strindbergian.") Helen Vendler's eminence would be revenged with the Paglian epithet "the Leona Helmsley of Harvard." Eve Kosofsky Sedgwick would be patronizingly credited with "pedestrian critical skills" but "the dogged determination of Richard Nixon on the rubber-chicken circuit."

Paglia's bitterness was not just sour grapes. Her own failure haunted her far less than her generation's. The baby boomers had burst onto the scene with such promise in the 1960s, but they had made a botch of the revolution, and it was no one's fault but their own. "Many of us, through folly, hubris, or mischance, have died or been left sleeping in the land of the Lotus-eaters," Paglia lamented. "America's current intellectual crisis originates in the tragic loss of the boldest and most innovative members of the 1960s generation." This decimation had a catastrophic effect on her own work—not on her career, that is, but on the quality of her scholarship—because all of the people with whom she should have been in dialogue had vanished from the conversation. As she tapped away in her attic writing studio, the only voice rattling around in her head was her own, and her TV's.

These wilderness years ended with the publication of *Sexual Personae* in 1990. Yale University Press had accepted the manuscript in 1985 without, one suspects, anticipating much in the way of sales. The hardcover sold a surprising seventeen thousand copies in its first year, and the New York publishing house Vintage bought the paperback rights for a rumored $65,000. That edition stayed on the *New York Times* bestseller list for five weeks. In a stroke of brilliant timing, soon after the book was published, Paglia had two op-eds that were widely syndicated, one on Madonna for *The New York Times* and one on date rape for *Newsday*. The latter was particularly provoking, especially when Paglia refused to back down from her position that " 'no' has always been, and always will be, part of the dangerous, alluring courtship ritual of sex and seduction." Her notoriety led Paglia to be profiled in *Spin*, *The Advocate*, and *New York* magazine, and lampooned repeatedly by the cheeky lads at *Spy*.

Through a combination of continuing good luck and instinctive media savvy, Paglia was able to parlay this initial burst of celebrity into a more lasting fame as a public intellectual. At a time when other academics tended to conduct their public arguments with polite decorum, her brawling Italian combativeness was refreshing. Nor was she modest in her selection of feud partners. On a media tour of Britain she got into a tabloid scrap with Princess Diana over a television program, presented by Paglia, featuring satirical cartoons depicting the princess in a Union Jack G-string. Journalists loved Paglia because she could always be counted on to give her interviewers the kind of provocative quotation they were looking for. *Spin* asked her about battered wives, and she mused that they stayed with their husbands because "everyone knows throughout the world that many of these working-class relationships where women get beat up have hot sex." The London *Observer* asked her about child pornography, and Paglia declared herself opposed to it only because it involved child labor and "the abolition of child labor was one of the great reform movements of the last 200 years."

Her constant jabs at feminism and other left-wing pieties made her many interviewers ask, Camille, doesn't this make you a conservative? Her response was always to point to her three favorite things: prostitution, pornography, and homosexuality. "I am a pornographer," she crowed, where else but in an article for *Playboy*. Thus were the seeds of her downfall revealed at the height of her success. It was sex that would prove how wrong she had been about men and women, about culture, about everything. Her line in the date rape controversy was always that feminists were naive in refusing to accept that sex could not be made un-dangerous. Fair enough. But her own record as a public intellectual—sex positive, gender-bending, pornography lauding, prostitute worshipping—would prove Paglia to have been at least as naive as her opponents, and in a more toxic way.

Historians of the twenty-fifth century with three paragraphs to give to the twenty-first in their textbooks will be more likely to mention the proliferation of pornography than any living president. It is almost impossible for people under thirty to understand how porn-saturated their world is compared with any other period in human history, the Rome of Heliogabalus not excepted. Any thirteen-year-old with a smartphone can watch video of almost any sex act he cares to, as often as he likes, for free and in total privacy. Technology cannot bear all the blame for this. The advent of streaming video in the early years of the twenty-first century would not have been such a rout for decency if the legal and cultural barriers against pornography had not been completely obliterated in what was, in retrospect, a remarkably short period of time.

Philip Larkin was right. It did begin with the end of the *Chatterley* ban. There had been other famous obscenity acquittals in history—*Ulysses, Howl, Madame Bovary,* an ironic case because Flaubert makes it clear that Emma herself was corrupted by novel reading—but it was *Lady Chatterley's Lover* more than any other book that left obscenity law as impotent as Sir Clifford in his wheelchair. The crucial change was the introduction of one deceptively simple principle, with one important corollary.

Charles Rembar was an ordinary New York lawyer who had never been involved in a real trial, with witnesses and cross-examinations as opposed to mere motions, when he was approached by Barnet Rosset of Grove Press to defend *Lady Chatterley's Lover* against the postmaster general's ban in 1959. Rosset was acting on the recommendation of Norman Mailer, who happened to be Rembar's cousin. Mailer remembered how well Charles had advised him during a tussle with his publishers over *The Naked and the Dead*. The compromise they eventually settled on, printing "fug" instead of "fuck," had been Rembar's suggestion. So was launched a long and eminent career as a First Amendment lawyer and champion of banned books.

In his memoir, *The End of Obscenity*, Rembar explains that his landmark successful defenses of *Lady Chatterley's Lover, Tropic of Cancer,* and *Fanny Hill* were all attributable to a single idea: "In 1956 the concept did not exist at all. In 1966 it was full grown and dominant. . . . The idea was this: no matter what the courts and the legislatures had traditionally deemed 'obscene' . . . the government could not suppress a book if it had merit as literature."

Artistic merit, far from being a defense, was considered an aggravating factor in some lower courts as late as 1965—a much more logical position to take, when you think about it. If an obscene work has artistic charms that make its pornographic content more seductive, so much the worse for everyone involved.

The corollary was that artistic merit could be subject to expert testimony. That effectively canceled almost all censorship at a stroke, for even in 1966 there was no work of art so repellent that it could not find a defender in some English department somewhere, and if there had been then, there wouldn't be today. A well-known professor at Swarthmore recently volunteered on his personal blog that he would, if the syllabus called for it, gladly teach a snuff film. An obvious fool, you might say, but nonetheless an expert to whose judgment a court would defer. In the British *Chatterley* case of 1960—a criminal case argued before a jury, unlike the American trial—five of the jurors were observed, during their swearing in, to "read with some difficulty or hesitancy." Those half-literate jurors could hardly have been expected to trust their own judgment of literary merit above that of a phalanx of Oxbridge professors.

Even Justice John Marshall Harlan, who could sign his name

without difficulty, thought that the professors had to be deferred to. As he wrote in his 1966 decision in the *Fanny Hill* case,

> A number of acknowledged experts in the field of literature testified that *Fanny Hill* held a respectable place in serious writing, and *unless such largely uncontradicted testimony is accepted as decisive* it is very hard to see that the "utterly without redeeming social value" test has any meaning at all [emphasis added].

"Before these cases"—Rembar means his dirty trio—"literary merit had occasionally been a factor in obscenity prosecutions, but a subordinate one." It was in the course of defending *Lady Chatterley* that Rembar first came up with the idea of interpreting the obscenity standard established by the Supreme Court in 1957 ("utterly without redeeming social value") as referring to literary merit. This defense proved successful in federal court and later, on behalf of *Fanny Hill*, in the Supreme Court itself. From then on, the idea that the government had a right to ban obscene books was a dead letter—with the English professors as much to blame as anyone. Incidentally, 1966 was also the year that the Roman Catholic Church withdrew the force of ecclesiastical law from the centuries-old Index of Forbidden Books, saying that it would thereafter "put its trust in the mature conscience of the faithful."

After that, the barriers fell fast. America traveled with remarkable speed the distance between raiding the offices of *The National Police Gazette* and allowing a nine-foot illuminated *Playboy* sign to adorn the skyline of Chicago. In 1968, Lyndon Johnson planted a time bomb that would go off during his successor's first term: the

President's Commission on Obscenity and Pornography. The commission's final report, which Nixon and Congress both hastily repudiated, suggested that antipornography laws should be repealed and that obscene videos might even be socially beneficial, "in allowing for a release of sexual tension." It was bad enough for them to be blasé about the legal obstacles as long as the logistical obstacles remained high and obtaining dirty pictures still meant going to a dingy part of town and risking embarrassment in the checkout line. As late as 1982, the videos advertised in the back of *Penthouse* still cost $100 each. Then came the VCR. Then came smartphones.

How did Americans themselves feel about this at the time? It is difficult to say, because the usual fractiousness of polling numbers is multiplied when the subject is sex. Around the time of the above-mentioned presidential commission, 73 percent of Americans were puritanical enough to say that gratuitous sex scenes in movies should "definitely not be allowed," but at least some of the same people must also appear among the nearly 60 percent who told pollsters that "adults should be allowed to read or see any explicit materials they want to." In the end, it did not matter what Americans *wanted*, in the democratic-deliberative sense. The onrushing debauch had a momentum of its own, the same way that the porn industry in the last twenty years has pushed itself into more and more extreme gonzo exploits as the only way to get any attention in a now overcrowded market. It's not what anybody wants, exactly. It's just the dynamic.

Camille Paglia, of all people, should have known that this escalating licentiousness would not come to rest in a happy equilibrium.

She had seen the same thing with her gay friends. Paglia was a fruit fly from an early age, as one might expect of a self-confessed Wildean. "What attracted me to gay men in college in the 1960s was their fierce independence of mind, their whiplash tongues, and their scorn for bourgeois decorum, saccharine sentimentality, and empty ideology." She joined with gusto in all their campiest pastimes, including pornography. "We've watched gay porn together and commented on the size of the actors' members," Bruce Benderson told *The Advocate*. Benderson and Paglia met when they were ten years old, growing up in Syracuse, New York. She credits him with being the only man whose knowledge of the films of Joan Crawford is more encyclopedic than her own.

This golden age of tagging along to drag bars and discussing the finer points of Bette Davis did not last. "I remember when the doors of the men's bars closed in my face," she recalled. "It was probably 1974; the hostility to a female presence was palpable. The reason: pitch-black orgy rooms and sex shows—chained men sodomized in slings—were coming into fashion." An attempt to pass in drag drew derisive laughter from the bouncers. It was a disillusioning moment, but one that should have been foreseen. Paglia might have been drawn to the gay scene for the esprit, or whatever, but her friends were in it for something simpler, and they were not about to shelve their desires for the sake of hospitality. Once disinhibition became the reigning ethos, its logic had to be carried to its end. License, like nature, abhors a vacuum.

After that experience, Paglia had no excuse for being naive. When the gay science fiction writer Samuel R. Delany took a curious female friend to his favorite Times Square porno theater in 1975, her first comment upon leaving was "There really *were* guys giving other guys blow jobs downstairs in the orchestra! I thought it was all going to be in dark corners." Paglia could have told her. Gay culture might seem delightfully insouciant from the outside, but she knew what was happening behind club doors. Later, she came to know how the whole story ended—in plague. And yet when she finally became famous, with two of her best friends dead from AIDS and the excesses of the bathhouse era tempered but by no means tamed, she persisted in arguing that the problem in America was too little sex, not too much.

At a certain point one can diagnose only willful blindness. In a curious coincidence, after Paglia made her name telling feminists to go back to their fainting couches when they complained about sexual harassment, she was commissioned by the British Film Institute to write a book-length monograph about *The Birds*, a film that featured the most notorious behind-the-scenes sexual harassment in cinematic history. Alfred Hitchcock tortured Tippi Hedren on the set of *The Birds*—either in lieu of making a pass at her or because his pass had been rejected, depending on whom you believe—to the point that Hedren collapsed and had to see a doctor. The BBC made a TV movie about the whole saga in 2012, starring Toby Jones and Sienna Miller. Paglia's book dispenses with the story in a single paragraph: "In my interview with her, Hedren rejected the widespread theories about Hitchcock's misogynous malice. She said of the attic scene, 'He felt very badly about it.'" This was the attic scene that had precipitated Hedren's collapse, when Hitchcock surreptitiously substituted live birds for the mechanical ones she had been expecting. Needless to say, Hedren does not tell it quite so forgivingly in her own memoir. Paglia simply cannot bring herself to admit that Hedren's goddess-like self-possession was powerless to save her from having her career ruined by a sexually jealous man.

Again and again Paglia has seen her rosy expectations of human sexuality run aground on harsh facts. "During the Sixties sexual revolution, I believed that, in a reformed future, prostitution would be unnecessary, since emancipated female desire would expand to meet men's needs." She concedes that things have not quite worked out that way. This has in no way diminished her enthusiasm for prostitution as something worth not only legalizing but positively defending. She sometimes sees streetwalkers on her way to work in Philadelphia in the early morning: " 'Pagan goddess!' I want to call out, as I sidle reverently by." Individual disillusionments pile up, and still her basic optimism is untouched.

"One cannot make any kind of firm line between high art and pornography," Paglia once told an interviewer. "Michelangelo is a pornographer." While Paglia was busy descanting on the erotic qualities of the *Pietà*, men under forty were developing erectile dysfunction at unprecedented rates from watching too much Pornhub. The average age at which a young person first sees pornography is now eleven, and what they see is far more depraved than what their parents or even older brothers grew up on. What would have been "soft core" ten years ago is now a Shakira music video. And still Paglia is blithe. In that very first op-ed about date rape for *Newsday* in 1991, she accused feminists of "sugar-coated Shirley Temple nonsense" and plumed herself on being hardheaded enough to admit that "aggression and eroticism are deeply intertwined." Shirley Temple she may not be, but in the end it is Paglia who underestimated the consequences that would follow when human desires were unleashed.

Now approaching her fourth decade of celebrity, Paglia soldiers on. Her act has not changed much since her heyday. Her third essay collection, *Free Women, Free Men*, dwelled on the same themes as her first two and even reprinted the same pieces—not just a handful of repeats, but a dozen. When a writer offers her public the same book three times in a row, she is either obsessed or graveled for matter. Paglia seems to be the latter. Her education equipped her to become a great critic, but at some point her development stalled. Her first book of original material since *Sexual Personae* was the annotated poetry anthology *Break, Blow, Burn* in 2005, and in 272 pages that book contains not one original insight. It is also written for the children's table. Accommodating the general reader is one thing, interrupting your exegesis of "Because I Could Not Stop for Death" to explain that tulle "is fine netting for veils and ballet costumes" is something else.

Then again, you did not have to be original to be a valuable soldier in the war on political correctness in the early 1990s. All you needed was a sharp pen and a nose for cant. A whole squadron of fighting pundits emerged in those years, and Paglia really was the best of them. Her only rival intellectually was Allan Bloom, and Bloom . . . he makes a big deal in *The Closing of the American Mind* of having been at Cornell during the Black Power takeover of Willard Straight Hall, notable in the history of campus unrest as the first occasion when the students were armed with guns. What Bloom fails to mention is that he was so distraught by the affair that at one point he became (as one historian puts it) "temporarily emotionally incapacitated"; that is, he was bawling his eyes out. He was thirty-eight years old at the time. Whatever else you want to say about Camille Paglia, she would never have been sidelined in the middle of a campus crisis by a hysterical crying jag.

Paglia was also a more acute critic than Bloom, because she realized that the so-called tenured radicals were not really radicals at all but apple-polishing class president types, or else plain hucksters. All the real radicals had flamed out on drugs or dropped out of academia after one rejection too many by timid hiring committees. The universities were abandoned to "toadying careerists, Fifties types who wave around Sixties banners to conceal their record of ruthless, beaverlike tunneling to the top." Paglia had every reason to take their success personally, because these colorless people had adopted the mantle that should rightfully have been hers. She, not they, had been a genuine rebel and paid the price in rejection by the establishment. These PC professors *were* the establishment. This grudge lent a certain zest to Paglia's punditry. She called them ignorant, she called them craven, she called them sex starved.

None of it made the slightest difference, because the levers Paglia and her comrades were yanking on so energetically were not connected to the engine fueling the PC craze. Just as stomach ulcers were belatedly discovered to be caused not by stress but by a humble bacterium, historians of the future may well discover that the real reason campuses erupt in fanaticism is the prosaic fact that the rest of us have started shoveling money at them. The first round in the 1960s took place at a time when the number of college students in America had increased by a factor of five in the space of three decades. Naturally this swollen demographic became conscious of itself as a bloc and wanted to throw its weight around, like new money. The administrators and professors had their heads turned, too, by newfound cultural importance and flush budgets, and so they let them.

In the 1990s comedy sequel, every last one of America's parents could have been convinced that colleges were all subliterate orgy dens, and political correctness would still have rolled on undaunted, because there was no chance those parents were going to let their children neglect to get a college degree. The credential was too important, and getting more important all the time. No matter how ridiculous particular institutions were made to look, college in general became only a bigger and bigger slice of the national economy. In the first hundred days of his presidency Barack Obama proposed spending $12 billion on community colleges, which, if it had passed Congress, would only have resulted in more states deciding that firemen and state troopers must learn how to put their footnotes in MLA format before we give them permission to save our lives. The effect that credential inflation has had on the professoriat is easy to imagine. When they see that they have the power to make a man who once would have been an adult with a wife and kid instead sit in a cage well into his midtwenties, taking creative writing from some goateed drudge, they don't worry whether they have the power to get away with a comparative bagatelle like gender-neutral pronouns.

The marginal students being tipped over the funnel into the college meat grinder in ever greater numbers aren't majoring in queer studies, of course. They have normal majors like psychology and education. It would be a mistake to conclude from this that horror stories from the frontiers of Lacanian theory are irrelevant, however, first of all because psychology and education are no less PC than the Wellesley women's studies department these days, if political correctness is measured by self-serious invocations of "diversity" and "privilege." Second, people with BAs in psychology from Nothingburger U. have a chip on their shoulder about having a college degree, because they are closer, socioeconomically, to the people who don't. They need to prove they are college educated, and the easiest way to do that is by being even more dogmatically progressive than those less anxious souls who went to proper liberal arts schools. Pouring more and more people into higher education does not dilute the influence of the PC wackos. Quite the opposite.

Paglia maintains that the solution to all this is for academia to rediscover its sense of purpose. "Scholarship is an ideal and a calling, not merely a trade or a living," she writes. "It has to recover its clerical or spiritual roots." The opposite advice would be more helpful, which is to say that a *deflating* of liberal education would do America a world of good. This fuzzy nonsense about academia being soul creating is piffle of a very recent vintage. The first ever professor of English literature at Oxford University, appointed in 1904, by the end of his career was writing to a friend, "God forgive us all! If I am accused on Judgment Day of teaching English literature, I shall plead that I never believed in it and that I maintained a wife and children." His cynicism is far healthier than the overblown panegyrics one reads in *The Chronicle of Higher Education*, which amount to nothing more than the same puffed-up veneration the Romantics used to claim on behalf of the Artist, reapplied to the Professor. At least the artists looked the part. Applied to the bureaucrats and busybodies of the modern university, the old reverential lines are just comical.

Paglia has written movingly about her days teaching Shakespeare and Sophocles to factory workers at the Sikorsky Aircraft plant outside New Haven, so she could hardly endorse a solution that involves ejecting so many working-class students from college life. When you ask the average humanities professor whether too many unready students might not be getting hustled into the matriculation office, he (or, statistically, she) will often wax populist: *everyone* deserves a chance to contemplate the big questions of life. Such big questions are indeed the stuff of literature and philosophy. But they are also the stuff of church. Religion has historically been the place where classes below the upper middle can air their ideas about meaning and seek to integrate them with a greater tradition. The nice thing about church is, it doesn't cost $50,000 a year.

S till, there are some things academia is good for. The beauties of great literature are accessible to anyone with a library card, whether they happen to have a college degree or not, but to the extent that the conversation across the ages is an ongoing one, it is being conducted in universities and a handful of magazines. True, it is a minority pastime. There are very few people whose pleasure, and fewer still whose employment, consists in debating the big books, but Paglia is one of them. It must therefore be with considerable dismay that she observes, if she is being honest with herself, that most of the people engaged in this enterprise today are too dumb for her to fight with.

Paglia discovered during her spats with the feminist establishment that an astonishing number of women's studies professors lack basic knowledge of how hormones work. The academics of the coming generations will be more ignorant still, if the quality of today's undergraduates is anything to go by. In one of her own English seminars at the University of the Arts in Philadelphia, Paglia was horrified to learn upon assigning the spiritual "Go Down, Moses" that "of a class of twenty-five students, only two seemed to recognize the name 'Moses.' . . . They did not know who he was." Lest you think this a function of the school's selectivity or lack thereof, a professor at one of the top University of California schools has told me, "I have had students who thought the printing press was invented after World War II, or who were surprised that Jesus was a Jew killed by Romans. This is at a school where the interquartile range of SAT verbal is 620–740."

Some of this is Paglia's fault, or the fault of the pop culture she lionizes. When the time comes to tabulate Paglia's personal moral record on this earth, it will have to take account of the fact that no public intellectual has argued more vehemently in defense of television, Hollywood, rock and roll, and other low entertainment. When *Harper's Magazine* wanted to do a clash-of-the-titans cover article in 1991 on the question of whether TV and movies had been good or bad for the culture, Paglia was the one chosen to argue in visual media's defense, opposite Neil Postman, author of *Amusing Ourselves to Death*. The exchange itself was a draw, but Paglia might well have felt that she had won that fight before it began. Postman's job title at the time was Paulette Goddard Chair of Media Ecology at NYU—the Paulette Goddard in question, of course, being the former Ziegfeld girl, Hollywood starlet, and third wife of Charlie Chaplin.

Richard Hoggart first suggested that England was "a democracy whose working people are exchanging their birthright for a mass of pin-ups" in 1957, when John Lennon was still debating whether to let Paul McCartney into the Quarrymen. The fact that pop culture's domination has only increased since then, combined with the fact that we are all still here and writing about it, has led some to conclude that these perennial forewarnings must be overblown. But that would be hasty. Observing the inability of even professional writers (academics, journalists, speechwriters, everybody) to meet the standards that prevailed in their respective fields two or three generations back, one has to consider the possibility that the doomsayers were right.

Alas, it is impossible to compare pop culture of today to culture of the past. The effect of pop culture has been to make it so that the best culture of a century ago now *has no equivalent*. There was once such a thing as high culture, and such a thing as folk culture. Neither exists today.

Paglia sidesteps this collapse of higher forms of culture into the popular by blurring the lines between them. "The glamorous, tawdry lives of Hollywood stars are the hero sagas of modern life," she writes, in far more elevated language than usually gets applied to *Us Weekly*. She once suggested abolishing the Nobel Prize in Literature due to the "declining importance of the written word in our age of mass media" and instead making it "a culture prize" for rock stars and film directors. Her greatest love, of all the arts of the twentieth century, is the golden age of Hollywood, which she regards not as a pleasant diversion but as one of the "three major eruptions of paganism" in Western culture, after the Renaissance and romanticism. Her pose on the cover of *Vamps and Tramps* is borrowed from Ursula Andress in *Dr. No*, the title of the volume's centerpiece essay ("No Law in the Arena") borrowed from *Ben-Hur*. Even *Sexual Personae*, her most scholarly work, has a title inspired by a movie, albeit one by Ingmar Bergman.

Paglia herself realizes that mass media has affected the workings of her brain in fundamental ways. "My generation's synapses are electronic and our circuitry hyperkinetic," she admits. "I have a psychedelic mind. It's because I grew up on rock and roll." When she said that (1992), she considered it a good thing—as well she might, considering that she produced the work that made her famous with her TV humming in the background as she wrote.

But something about seeing the long-term effects of mass culture on her students has made her reconsider in the years since, if only tentatively. The twentieth anniversary edition of *Amusing Ourselves to Death*, released by Penguin in 2005, features the following blurb:

> As a fervent evangelist of the age of Hollywood, I publicly opposed Neil Postman's dark picture of our media-saturated future. But time has proved Postman right. He accurately foresaw that the young would inherit a frantically all-consuming media culture of glitz, gossip, and greed.
>
> —CAMILLE PAGLIA

The introduction to *Sexual Personae* explains that the book the reader is holding is in fact only the first volume of a two-part work. The second volume would apply the literary themes of the first to "movies, television, sports, and rock music." By the time *Vamps and Tramps* was released in 1994, Paglia's story on this sequel was that it "was completed in 1981 but is currently being revised to incorporate the thousands of notecards that have accumulated over the intervening decade and a half."

No such volume has yet appeared. It may be, as Paglia has elsewhere indicated, that she has simply said most of what she had to say on pop culture in her occasional essays. But Paglia's scholarly work has always been at a qualitatively higher level than her journalism. Could it be that when she took her critical intelligence, that great big brain schooled in New Criticism and close reading at the best English program in the Ivy League, and applied it to popular culture, she discovered that the object of her attention simply could not bear up under it?

However discomfiting Susan Sontag found the suggestion that Camille Paglia deserved to be considered her heir, the parallels between them are self-evident. Even this oedipal sparring with a forerunner was something Sontag herself had done, in her case with Mary McCarthy, whose position as the beautiful-yet-brilliant doyenne of the New York little magazines she had assumed in the 1960s. When McCarthy traveled to North Vietnam in 1968, Sontag arranged to travel the same route a few weeks later, and their two travelogues were published almost simultaneously under near-identical titles, *Hanoi* and *Trip to Hanoi*. Sontag even took over McCarthy's theater column for *Partisan Review* in 1963. When the two women were first introduced, McCarthy is reported to have said, "So you're the one who is supposed to be the next me."

With the perspective of time, it is clear that in the Sontag-Paglia rivalry, Paglia prevailed. She was a better critic and a better writer at the sentence level, and she had the guts to come out as a lesbian, which Sontag never did, not even in her later years when everyone knew about Annie Leibovitz and it wouldn't have cost her anything. But if Sontag descended like a submarine into a Mariana Trench of faux profundity, Paglia's work, taken as a whole, seems less profound than it should be.

Paglia and Sontag both earned PhDs, something that Mary McCarthy never had but always wished she did. (In the autobiographical novel *A Charmed Life* she gives her stand-in character a PhD in philosophy.) Yet even without that credential, McCarthy went further and achieved more as a writer than either of them. It is her work that stands most chance of still being read a hundred years from now. If her latter successor would like an explanation for this curious fact, she may find the answer in Mary McCarthy's maxim that writing about mass culture for a mass audience should be avoided, as being too much like "the mirror on the ceiling of the whorehouse."

6

AL SHARPTON

What kind of leader is the Reverend Al Sharpton? In the book he wrote for his 2004 presidential campaign, *Al on America*, he explains that there are two kinds: "There are those who are thermometers. A thermometer records the temperature. And there are those who are thermostats; they change the temperature." Ten years later, in his second memoir, *The Rejected Stone*, he supplements this metaphor with a citation from the book *Leadership* by the American historian James MacGregor Burns, which also divides leaders into two types. As Sharpton summarizes Burns's dichotomy, "A transactional leader will do and say whatever he or she needs to get elected, while a transformational leader tries to change the course of history and make decisions that are moral, just, and right."

Sharpton, of course, sees himself as transformational and his rivals as transactional. "I'm trying to transform society; they're trying to move up in society." He compares it to the situation that existed in the 1960s. "While Dr. King was fighting against segregation, there were other black leaders at the time who accommodated segregation because they got something out of it. They got elected, but they didn't make society better."

It's not just Sharpton. Every boomer gets indignant at the suggestion that their generation's effect on race relations has been anything short of transformational. It is their overwhelming rebuttal to the (you will by now surely agree) otherwise unanswerable case against them. Whatever else we might be guilty of, they say, we did civil rights. In a slight fudge of the chronology, boomers give themselves credit for the legal revolutions of the mid-1960s, which, unless they were freedom riding at age ten, is a stretch. Al Sharpton really *was* involved in civil rights as a tween, so he has a better sense of the time line and of himself as an heir, rather than a member, of the King generation. But for the broader public, the equation has settled into our collective mind: boomers = 1960s = civil rights.

A better test of the boomers' record would obviously be the decades when they were in charge. What has happened to race relations in the years since Dr. King was shot in 1968, or better yet since the first nationally observed Martin Luther King Day in 1986? A cynic might say that things have become, to use Sharpton's terms, more transactional. Civil rights leaders used to draw our eyes to the view from the mountaintop. Now it's about the bottom line, getting a fat consent decree out of Texaco, or creating more jobs in campus diversity offices. "They bash me at Fox News, but they sponsor my conference," Sharpton boasted, accurately, at the 2012 get-together of his group the National Action Network, which over the years has received millions of dollars not just from Rupert Murdoch's News Corp but from companies such as Best Buy, Chrysler, Citigroup, General Motors, Pfizer, Verizon, and Walmart.

But the truth is that there are good transactional leaders as well as bad ones, and today there are far *fewer* of the good kind than there used to be. The boomers persuaded everybody that transformational leadership was the only kind worth admiring, which left transactional leadership, the kind that bargains and compromises, with a low reputation that it did not deserve. Sometimes transactional leadership can be the more noble type. The transformational mentality looks at opposition and sees nothing but reactionary holdouts who don't deserve to be accommodated, only defeated. A transactional leader sees potential allies whose cooperation could be gained if their concerns were placated.

If crass racial shakedowns have flourished in the last three decades, it is not because the transactional tradition of racial leadership has prevailed. Quite the opposite. It has been nearly abandoned. Just as the history of Communism teaches us that abolishing capitalism doesn't put an end to exploitation, the discrediting of transactional leadership has taught us that when the art of bargaining with your opponents is abolished, other forms of extracting concessions from them inevitably take its place.

Some of the boomers profiled in this book were selected because their lives illustrate some generational arc. Not Sharpton. His life barely has an arc to it at all. He decided in elementary school that he wanted to be a preacher and activist, and that is what he has been ever since. He never had to adapt his personality to the pressure of being in the public eye, because he has never been out of it.

One cannot say Sharpton's ambition was the result of his father's having left when he was ten years old, because his ordination as a

Pentecostal "boy preacher" predates it, but family breakup certainly redoubled whatever psychological drives were already present. The abandonment was particularly harrowing due to its incestuous nature: Al Sharpton Sr. knocked up his wife's eighteen-year-old daughter from her first marriage and left to set up house with her. Eventually middle sister Cheryl was invited to live in their new household. Al junior was not. He and his mother were forced to relocate to Brownsville, which meant moving from a ten-bedroom house with a two-car garage in a middle-class suburb in Queens to living in a black ghetto and subsisting on welfare.

That was in 1964. Sharpton first came to national attention in 1985 leading marches against the subway vigilante Bernie Goetz. The years in between were not spent on politics, though the skills he developed later proved politically useful. Mostly he spent the 1970s touring with James Brown. "Reverend, I need you to stay on the road with me now, I don't trust no one else but you counting my money," was the Godfather of Soul's way of explaining to Sharpton why he needed him. Sharpton served as tour manager, booking agent, and surrogate son; Brown's son Teddy, who was Sharpton's age, had died in a car accident in 1973 soon after Sharpton joined the entourage.

Traveling on the road with Brown taught Sharpton as much about business as it did about showmanship. Brown was a shrewd negotiator. He was booked to play a concert in the Congo right before the famous "Rumble in the Jungle" between Muhammad Ali and George Foreman. On the way to the airport, he realized he hadn't been paid his full fee yet and told Don King's people to get him his $100,000 in cash or he wouldn't get on the plane. When the show was finished, he had Sharpton meet him at the airport in

Kinshasa to fly out before the fight was even over. "Reverend, how many times do I have to tell you that this is a business?" he explained. "I did my show, I made my money, I got things to do."

Sharpton was never entirely removed from politics, even in his touring years. In 1971, he founded his own organization, the National Youth Movement, which he used to pressure black artists like Tina Turner, Lionel Richie, and Michael Jackson to hire black promoters for their tours. He called the dominance of white promoters a form of "business apartheid." He also continued to preach every Sunday. Sharpton is not one of those civil rights leaders for whom "Reverend" is a courtesy title. He is a real preacher, and his sermons are real sermons, not veiled political speeches. Preaching kept him connected to the grass roots and what was happening at street level during the racially turbulent 1970s.

Combining ministry and politics is a long tradition in the black community. One of the most famous examples was Sharpton's first political mentor, a man who was his idol even before James Brown, from whom he borrowed the habit of wearing a gold medallion around his neck, a man whose transformational style of politics frequently put him into collision with the transactionalists at Tammany Hall: the Reverend Adam Clayton Powell, Jr.

The purest example of the transactional tradition in American politics is big-city machine politics, which, coincidentally or not, has also been the type of American politics most favorable to the advancement of the poor. In 1910, when Booker T. Washington toured Europe for his book *The Man Farthest Down* to see if he could find a group of people worse off than Southern blacks, he concluded that the worst-off people in the world were Sicilian peasants. Slaving away for their feudal lords, the Sicilians were fed, clothed, and housed worse than sharecroppers and less likely to be able to read. Yet when these degraded Italian immigrants arrived in Manhattan, they discovered that Tammany Hall was eager to find them housing, give them money, listen to their troubles, and ask for nothing in return but their votes. More than any other institution in American history, with the possible exception of the Roman Catholic Church, the big-city machines were genuinely egalitarian.

It wasn't just welfare the machines offered. They were schools of leadership. A ward heeler, the machine's lowest-ranking foot soldier, would typically be responsible for a neighborhood of a few hundred families. His job was to turn his voters out on Election Day, which meant he couldn't just be a loudmouth but had to be someone his neighbors would heed. It also meant he had to spot any burgeoning discontents before they started eroding his support. That was the service he provided, in exchange for the turkeys his superiors gave him to hand out at Christmas: a line of communication between the people and their government. When a machine mayor asked himself what his citizens thought, he actually knew, not from polls, but from this informational respiratory system.

There were never many black machine politicians. Partly this was because black migration to the North peaked at a time when the machines were already dying for other reasons, like the federalization of welfare programs. Partly it was because black voter turnout was consistently lower than other groups'. Tammany would have loved to add blacks to its coalition as far back as 1898, when it created the outreach group the United Colored Democracy, led by Edward E. Lee, head bellman of the Murray Hill Hotel. Lee flourished as a Tammany power broker, despite being a lifelong illiterate, but black turnout remained stubbornly low. In the 1926 election, Harlem's population of 225,000 cast fewer than 16,000 votes.

But Lee was far from the only black boss. In the 1950s, if you asked the man on the street to name the most powerful politician in Harlem, most would have said the Reverend Adam Clayton Powell, Jr. He was young Al Sharpton's hero from the day he saw Powell's face staring from a bookstore shelf and saved up ninety-nine cents to buy the book, "excited that someone had written a book about a minister."

Between 1944 and 1970, the people of Harlem elected Adam Clayton Powell to Congress every two years like clockwork, even when he was under indictment, or when he refused to pay a court libel judgment and couldn't set foot in his own district for fear of being thrown in jail for contempt. When his corruption became so blatant that the House of Representatives refused to seat him in 1967, a special election was held, and his constituents reelected him again. The source of his power was his charisma. His constituents didn't care if he gave his girlfriends no-show jobs on the federal payroll, or took extravagant taxpayer-funded junkets to Europe, or cheated on his taxes, as long as he kept smiling and never apologized.

Powell was the most famous politician in Harlem, but insiders might still have said that its most powerful politician was J. Raymond Jones, known as the Harlem Fox. Jones was born on the Caribbean island of St. Thomas and immigrated to New York in the 1920s, finding work as a railroad porter. He joined Tammany Hall and rose through the ranks the old-fashioned way, diligently serving the organization in unglamorous backstage positions and making shrewd alliances. In 1964, he attained Tammany's highest office, head of the New York County (Manhattan) Democratic Party, making him the first and only black boss of Tammany Hall. From behind the scenes, he sponsored the political careers of such rising black leaders as Constance Baker Motley and the future mayor David Dinkins.

Powell and Jones were opposites in every way, and for a while their complementary virtues made them a good team. When Powell split from the machine in 1958 and had to run for his congressional seat as an independent, Jones managed his campaign. When Tammany loyalists posing as volunteers showed up at Powell's campaign headquarters offering to help collect signatures, Jones spotted their sabotage attempt right away. The "volunteers" were going to turn in fraudulent forms that would get Powell's petitions invalidated by the election board. Jones pretended to believe them, let them waste their time, then threw their forms in the trash.

Which of the two men was more powerful? Powell had celebrity, but on the other hand he was widely disliked by his colleagues. He had a bad habit of betraying his allies. In 1960, Powell accused Martin Luther King and Bayard Rustin of being "captives" of socialist interests, and his red-baiting forced King to eject Rustin, who did have left-wing ties, from his inner circle. Powell crossed party lines to endorse Eisenhower for president in 1956 (possibly in exchange for the Justice Department dropping its investigation into his taxes), and his Democratic friends accused him of changing his convictions for personal gain. "That is a complete lie," he replied in a radio interview. "I didn't have any convictions to change." His white colleagues in the House despised him as a charlatan and a criminal. He was not likely to rise high in the committee structure.

Powell served in Congress for more than fifteen years before he finally got his big break. Speaker of the House Sam Rayburn wanted his old friend Lyndon Johnson to get the presidential nomination in 1960, and he told Ray Jones that if he could deliver the New York delegation on the first two ballots, Rayburn would appoint Adam Clayton Powell chairman of the powerful House Education and Labor Committee. It was from this position that Powell shaped welfare policy during the Great Society, and also directed significant pork to his home district. He would never have been given the chairmanship in the first place if not for Rayburn's deal with Jones. The charismatic celebrity owed his position of power to the backroom dealer.

But it was Powell, not Jones, whom the young Al Sharpton idolized. As a boy Sharpton persuaded his sister to take him up to the Abyssinian Baptist Church on 138th Street to see Powell preach. "He was very tall, erect, almost majestic," Sharpton remembered later. "I thought I had seen God." He was even more delighted when, after the service, Powell recognized him as "Alfred Sharpton, boy preacher from F. D. Washington's church in Brooklyn." Powell allowed the boy preacher to pal around with his entourage as he schmoozed parishioners, went on Dick Cavett's show, and generally lived the high life. Powell was Sharpton's first surrogate father figure, a role model whose example would inspire his own career. Jones he had probably never heard of.

In his 1996 memoir, *Go and Tell Pharaoh*, Sharpton claims that Adam Clayton Powell was "for a long time . . . the only black congressman." In fact, Powell was never the only black congressman.

He was preceded and nearly outlasted by Representative William Dawson of Illinois, the highest-ranking African American in the Cook County machine of Chicago's mayor, Richard J. Daley.

Daley was America's transactional leader par excellence. At a time when political scientists were declaring machine politics obsolete, Daley was the undisputed boss of a machine that was stronger than it had been at any time in its century of existence. The Chicago machine's exceptional longevity was partly due to its ability to assimilate new groups, including blacks. They arrived in large numbers later than the Irish and the Poles, but Daley assumed they would rise by the same methods, and indeed Dawson was hardly the only black man to hold high office in the Daley organization. When Martin Luther King came to Chicago in 1966, it was a showdown not just between two men but between two very different types of politics, one pragmatic, the other symbolic.

The Chicago Freedom Movement, as King's initiative was called, was supposed to be the Southern Christian Leadership Conference's triumphant follow-up to Selma. It was also meant to signal the civil rights movement's pivot to the North. In January 1966, Dr. King moved with Coretta and the children into an apartment in North Lawndale on Chicago's West Side. He officially kicked off the campaign in June by marching from Soldier Field to city hall and, in the manner of his namesake, nailing (actually taping) his list of demands to the door. The demands were a mixed assortment, from minority hiring in city departments to a citizen review board for police brutality. "But for our primary target," King declared, "we have chosen open housing."

Housing was chosen because it was thought to be a straightforward northern analogue to lunch counters: if I can eat where I want, I should be able to live where I want. But housing in Chicago was not so simple. More than any other northern city, Chicago prided itself on being a "city of neighborhoods." The nationality of your neighborhood determined whether your local church was a St. Patrick's or a St. Stanislaus, what kind of sausage the butcher sold, and a million other things. Residents were sensitive to encroachment even by other white ethnics. Complicating matters was the fact that Chicago's black population had exploded since World War II, more than tripling between 1940 and 1965 from 8 percent to 28 percent. White residents feared that the city was being expected to accommodate the entire black population of Mississippi, who apparently had all decided to pick up and move. A certain amount of flux in the neighborhood map was expected, but King seemed to be demanding that the borders of the South Side be expanded indefinitely.

Poor conditions in Chicago's black neighborhoods were not entirely the result of overcrowding either. On the South Side, maintenance workers had garbage thrown at them from windows so often they started wearing hard hats on jobs in the neighborhood. Welfare workers were forbidden to take the stairs in South Side buildings because they were so likely to be assaulted and robbed there. Gangs extorted money from local businesses and even local churches. When the Atlanta civil rights leader Andrew Young first visited the Kings in their Chicago apartment, he noticed that the street corners were full of drug dealers and all the elevators smelled like urine. How would open housing address problems like that?

When the SCLC announced that they were coming to Chicago, local black leaders held a press conference to tell them their help was not welcome. These were no Uncle Toms but accomplished men like

Dr. Joseph H. Jackson, president of the five-million-member National Baptist Convention, and Ralph Metcalfe, the Olympic track and field athlete and four-term congressman. Many ordinary black Chicagoans were equally loyal to the machine. "When I first came to Chicago, me and my family had nothing but the rags on our back," one man told a researcher who asked why he supported Daley. "My precinct captain got us into public housing and some welfare until I could find a job. The precinct captain still comes around to check on things. So when I vote Democratic I'm voting for him—my precinct captain."

King protégé Hosea Williams boasted that the SCLC's voter drive would register 100,000 new black voters in time for the 1967 mayoral election. It fell short by more than 90 percent, registering fewer than 10,000, and Daley was reelected with 73 percent of the vote. "The Negroes of Chicago have a greater feeling of powerlessness than I ever saw," Williams lamented. He was from Attapulgus, Georgia, where there were no big-city bosses or even Irish Catholics, and he did not realize how different northern cities were from the Deep South he knew. The truth was that the Chicago Freedom Movement fell flat because blacks in Chicago *did* have power. (On another occasion, Hosea Williams disrupted Mass at St. Patrick's Cathedral in New York for a "preach-in," not knowing how offensive the stunt would be, and all the liberal Catholic priests in the city who had been working with the SCLC suddenly withdrew their support. Sharpton, who was working for the SCLC at the time, recalls the gaffe in his memoir.)

King described fighting with Daley as like "punching a pillow." The mayor accommodated as many of the SCLC's demands as he possibly could and did it with a smile. "When it was a battle cry to end the slums, the rats and roaches and all that. . . . Daley sent out all his inspectors and poisoned rats left and right. Then held press conferences," one activist remembered. Getting garbage picked up, building parks, repairing windows in housing projects—this stuff was Machine Politics 101. Daley was unwilling to destroy Chicago's unique ecosystem of ethnic neighborhoods, but everything else on King's list was just good politics. The Chicago Freedom Movement has gone down in history as a failure for the civil rights movement, but the real lesson was that for the average black citizen of Chicago, Daley's method of politics simply had more to offer.

Only one person came out of the SCLC's year in Chicago looking good, and that was Jesse Jackson, destined to become Sharpton's third surrogate father figure after Adam Clayton Powell and James Brown. When the SCLC dropped housing as its signature issue in 1967, it shifted to focus on getting northern businesses to hire more blacks. The jobs program was called Operation Breadbasket, and Jesse Jackson was put in charge of it. It was as a teen organizer for Breadbasket that Sharpton first met Jackson, making it an important landmark in Sharpton's life and also the civil rights campaign from which he learned the most.

Breadbasket's method was simple. Any Chicago company that failed to meet a workforce quota of 20 percent blacks would be gently informed of the need to hire more. Businesses that did not cooperate would be hit with picketing and boycotts. Negotiations ended in a "covenant" between the owner and Breadbasket. The Walgreens covenant in 1970, for example, pledged the company to hire 385 blacks over eighteen months, conduct "sensitivity seminars," purchase more products from black-owned suppliers, and submit periodic reports to Breadbasket to prove its compliance with the deal.

Interestingly, if Breadbasket had tried these tactics only a few decades earlier, courts would have considered them illegal. Boycotts, except in limited circumstances, were considered unfair commercial interference, and victimized owners could sue organizers for damages. In a landmark case in 1934, the Harlem agitator Sufi Abdul Hamid, also known as Black Hitler for his vocal support for the Third Reich, launched a boycott against the A. S. Beck shoe store on 125th Street demanding that it hire more blacks on its sales staff. A New York judge ruled the picket unlawful, not because store patrons had been violently assaulted (though they had been), but because Hamid and his picketers had no connection to the store. If it had been a protest by black Beck's employees demanding better treatment, that would have been a labor dispute and thus protected by the Norris-LaGuardia Act. But this was a conspiracy against a lawful business by a third party seeking to impose its political preferences. Even a peaceful boycott would have been illegal.

Perhaps this was why Jesse Jackson insisted on referring to Breadbasket's method as "withdrawal of patronage." "We don't use the word 'boycott,'" he said, "we just are not going to cooperate with evil." His activities skirted legality enough as it was. He was known to use the Blackstone Rangers, the South Side's most notorious gang, to intimidate grocery store owners into cooperating with him. Young men awaiting trial for robbery and murder were given paid positions in Breadbasket firms as management trainees and even security guards. Employers were not always happy with the way their "covenants" worked out in practice, but there was little they could do. One manager at the firm National Tea, who was black himself, said that his new contractors charged as much as five times more for their services but "many took the attitude that since Breadbasket put them in, there wasn't a damn thing we could do about their falling down on the job."

Jackson's success with Breadbasket vaulted him into a rivalry with the Reverend Ralph Abernathy, who had taken over the SCLC after King's assassination. Abernathy was uncharismatic as a speaker and autocratic as a leader, so there was demand both inside and outside the organization for someone else to step into the role as Dr. King's successor. Jackson thought he would be a good fit. Unfortunately, he made himself vulnerable through his sloppy financial practices. Abernathy caught Jackson funneling Breadbasket money to a separate organization under his personal control, and in 1971 Jackson was suspended from the SCLC. He resigned to start his own group, Operation PUSH (People United to Save Humanity).

It was probably time for Jackson to leave the SCLC anyway. Although he was born in South Carolina, Jackson came north to attend Chicago Theological Seminary in 1964 and adapted to the city in a way that the older Southern pastors of the SCLC never did. When Jackson first moved to Chicago, he actually had a private meeting with Mayor Daley, thanks to a letter of introduction from North Carolina's governor, Terry Sanford. Daley offered Jackson a job as a tollbooth agent, which he declined. The offer wasn't meant as an insult. The mayor was probably testing whether the glib young man in his office was willing to pay his dues, to serve before attempting to lead. In his seminary studies, Jackson soon became known for cutting corners on assignments, for example refusing to turn in written sermons for his preaching course because he preferred to extemporize. "You have to understand, I'm special," he told one professor—which is to say that Daley wasn't wrong to want to test Jackson's capacity for humility. Abernathy probably wished he had done the same.

Jackson has been such an innovative civil rights leader partly because of this gift for shortcuts, one reason he has been able to organize more effectively and on a larger scale than his rivals. Unfortunately, many of his shortcuts have been around the democratic process. Consider the way he finally managed to do what the SCLC never could: defeat Mayor Daley.

At the 1972 Democratic National Convention in Miami Beach, Daley was one of the most powerful party leaders in the room, having just been reelected for an unprecedented fifth term by a forty-point margin. But the McGovern Commission reforms of 1971 had changed the rules for selecting convention delegates. Each delegation now had to include a certain number of women, minorities, and people under thirty. Jesse Jackson lodged a complaint with the credentials committee that the Illinois delegation was not diverse enough under the new rules, and by a vote of 71 to 61, the credentials committee agreed. Daley accused Jackson of "disenfranchising over 900,000 voters who elected the Illinois delegates," but he was nevertheless forced to endure the humiliation of seeing his delegates ejected and Jackson's group seated in their place.

Jackson's ploy was blatantly undemocratic. The whole point of machine politics was always that you have only as much power as you deserve. Daley asked people who came into his office whom they represented and how many votes they could sway in their local assembly district, not because he was trying to give them a hard time, but because that was his way of testing whether someone represented an actual constituency. Lots of people claim to know what the people want. Democracy is how we know which of those people are telling the truth.

Jesse Jackson's career—indeed, the whole civil rights movement after 1970—has been dedicated to circumventing that democratic system. When Barack Obama was a young community organizer, he would visit local politicians and get the old Chicago brush-off: "Don't send me nobody that nobody sent." Five years later, he came back to town as a young lawyer and sued Citibank for alleged racial discrimination in its lending practices and won hundreds of thousands of dollars for black loan applicants. Compared with a payday like that, community organizing was a waste of time.

No one in civil rights is better at extracting large sums from big corporations than Jesse Jackson, which is why Al Sharpton spent so much time studying him. Jackson's method is like Operation Breadbasket on a larger scale. He chooses a company and, if possible, waits for a moment when it will be legally vulnerable, like a merger or an IPO. He then makes an accusation of racial discrimination, at which point the company has two choices. It can take its chances with bad press and a lawsuit, or it can come to an agreement with Jackson. That agreement can involve making a donation to one of his nonprofits, putting one of his friends on the board, giving a franchise contract to one of his family members, or any combination of the above.

The difference between this scheme and Breadbasket is that in Breadbasket businesses complied because they knew that black consumers would listen to Jackson when he called for a boycott. Now it is the Equal Employment Opportunity Commission that businesses are afraid of. No longer does Jackson need to have a following of ordinary people who find his accusations of racism credible. The hammer of antidiscrimination law is enough.

This is the tactic Sharpton has adopted for his National Action Network, just as he learned Breadbasket tactics from Jackson as a teen organizer in the 1970s. In 1998, Sharpton accused both Pepsi and Macy's of racist practices. Within months, Pepsi hired him as an adviser at $25,000 a year, a position he held for a decade, and Macy's sponsored NAN's annual conference. General Motors wrote its first check to NAN in 2007, shortly after Sharpton threatened GM with a boycott over the closing of a black-owned dealership in the Bronx.

Sharpton became so adept that he eventually came into conflict with his old mentor. In 2011, Comcast had been seeking approval for its merger with NBC Universal for two years. The swing vote on the Federal Communications Commission did not approve the merger until after Comcast signed a memorandum of understanding with NAN and two other civil rights groups. That memo agreed to give a longtime NAN board chairman a seat on Comcast's new minority advisory council, among other steps to promote diversity. Jesse Jackson had opposed the merger, which was controversial because of the size of the resulting media behemoth. A few months after the merger was approved, Sharpton was given his own show on MSNBC.

The anticorruption watchdog the National Legal and Policy Center has diligently documented Sharpton's most visible shakedowns, but it is not easy even for close observers to get the full story on Sharpton's finances. Conveniently timed fires have twice destroyed Sharpton's financial records, in 1997 during his run for New York City mayor and in 2003 just before his presidential campaign. His closest brush with legal trouble was being indicted in 1989 for stealing more than $250,000 from the National Youth Movement. After a trial in which the prosecution called eighty witnesses and the defense called none, a predominantly black jury acquitted him of all charges. Since then, the IRS and the state of New York have occasionally billed him for back taxes running into the millions, but Sharpton has negotiated a settlement with authorities each time.

In some ways the Jackson-Sharpton method of activism may seem like an improvement on the old Breadbasket method. Why bother organizing a boycott when persuading a regulator to threaten a business deal can get you what you want in half the time? But the tedious work cut out by this more efficient system turned out, in retrospect, to be essential to the democratic process.

Not many people know that if Congress had not passed the Civil Rights Act of 1964, Chief Justice Earl Warren was prepared to step in with a Supreme Court decision that would have accomplished much the same thing. The cases *Bell v. Maryland* and *Barr v. City of Columbia* involved sit-in protests at private lunch counters and hinged on whether the owners' actions in removing the protesters were unconstitutional under the Fourteenth Amendment the way they would have been if the restaurants had been government property.

Chief Justice Warren thought so. He believed the public/private distinction collapsed the moment the owner called the police to eject the protesters from his store. "To say that the policy is merely 'private' ignores the fact that without the State it could not survive," he wrote in an unreleased draft opinion. The NAACP lawyer in *Bell* went further. "The choice of the proprietor was not an authentically private decision," he told the Court, "but was influenced by the custom of the community, [which] was to some significant extent . . . influenced by the historic pattern of Maryland laws." Not just the man's deeds but even his opinions were a form of state action, the NAACP was claiming.

Warren deliberately withheld the Court's decisions on the sit-in cases until Congress acted on the civil rights bill, at which point the cases became moot. Would it have made a difference to history if Southern lunch counters had been integrated by a Supreme Court decision in March rather than a federal law in July? Constitutionally, there would have been a new precedent dissolving the difference between public and private action. More important, it would have robbed the American people of the chance to make a *democratic* statement on segregation. The give-and-take of legislative negotiations left the 1964 bill with some flaws that civil rights advocates were unhappy with, like its weak enforcement provisions (later strengthened in 1972). Those had been the price of getting moderates to vote yes. But to have a law with democratic legitimacy, it was a price worth paying.

Consider the counterexample of busing. There was an issue, if ever there was one, where the transformational leaders had their way and the transactional leaders were left out in the cold, along with any kind of democratic accountability. If a machine boss like Boston's John "Honey Fitz" Fitzgerald, President John F. Kennedy's grandfather and namesake, had been in charge of integrating Boston's schools, he would have done it gradually, balancing the interests of various wards against one another, the same way that Catholics and Protestants quarreled and compromised for decades over public funding for parochial schools. Instead, Judge Arthur Garrity decreed that South Boston's children would be bused to Roxbury and vice versa, and if you didn't like it, he would send in the National Guard.

The transactional compromisers were routed by the victorious thermostats. But were their methods a success? In September 1956, the House Committee on the District of Columbia held nine days of hearings on how D.C.'s schools had fared since integration was implemented overnight in the fall of 1954. (Because D.C. was under federal control, there was no foot-dragging as there was in other districts after *Brown*.) The testimony given at those hearings does not sound like a success.

At Roosevelt High School, which went from all white to fifty-fifty, disciplinary incidents quadrupled. The principal canceled the girls' cheerleading team because the new students were making so many lewd remarks to the girls at basketball games. That same principal had held an assembly the spring before integration where she told her students about a Japanese girl from an internment camp who had attended Roosevelt during World War II and how they must welcome the new students as their predecessors had welcomed her. But even she was disillusioned after driving past neighborhood swimming pools and playgrounds suddenly devoid of white children and being told in explanation, "We can't go over there. We get beat up." A teacher at McKinley High told the committee of a girl who was sexually assaulted by a black classmate and "her first reaction . . . was that it should be reported to the police," but school administrators instructed her to hush it up.

Teachers in white schools had been told to assume that their new students would be on roughly the same academic level as their old ones. Instead, they found tenth graders who couldn't write their own names and sixth graders who couldn't find Washington on a map—even though, prior to integration, the district's black and white schools had had equal budgets, fairly equal facilities, and the same salaries for teachers. With the best will in the world, it is not possible to teach tenth-grade English when half the class is ready for *Julius Caesar* and half the class has never heard of Rome. Nevertheless, when superintendent Carl F. Hansen introduced a four-tier academic tracking system to try to save the educations of those students, black and white, who were achieving at grade level, the liberal judge Skelly Wright struck it down as unconstitutional.

The transcripts of the House committee hearing, which run for nearly five hundred pages, are a vivid illustration of why, even on its own terms, judicially mandated integration was a failure. The D.C. public school system went from 36 percent white in 1955 to less than 10 percent white two decades later, a situation that persists today.

This failure was entirely due to the absence of transactional leadership. Those compromisers and accommodators might have denied the liberals some victories, but they would have made sure that the victories they did win were not Pyrrhic. If academic achievement among black students was not such as to make integration into the same classrooms feasible, they might have started by integrating those students who were academically prepared and devoted remedial funds to those who were not. They might have phased in their integration plan starting with 1954's kindergarteners. They might have met white parents' concerns about school discipline with enforcement measures that would have ensured their children could use playgrounds without getting their heads kicked in—surely a request no more unreasonable than that the Little Rock Nine should be able to walk to school without being pelted with rocks, no matter how many National Guardsmen it took to guarantee their safety. Because transactional leaders were sidelined, these compromises were never made.

Transformational leaders can let their rhetoric run away with them in a way transactional leaders, tethered to reality, can't. Even today Sharpton does not apologize for his role in promoting the Tawana Brawley hoax of 1987, where a black teenager falsely claimed to have been gang-raped over a period of several days by white law enforcement officials. It took the accused men a year to clear their names; one committed suicide. Brawley nevertheless remains a potent symbol of Sharpton's willingness to challenge white authority even against overwhelming odds.

Sharpton defends himself by saying that he will never apologize for trusting a vulnerable young woman in obvious distress. That's fair enough, if he looked into Tawana's eyes and saw the pain of generations of suffering black womanhood, but when he held his first march on Brawley's behalf, he *hadn't* looked into her eyes at all. The two had never met. When he held his first march in Teaneck, New Jersey, on behalf of the teenager Phillip Pannell, who was shot after firing his gun at a police officer pursuing him on foot, Sharpton didn't even know Pannell had been armed when he was killed.

The boy's family had neglected to mention that detail. Even after he learned about Pannell's gun, Sharpton left it out of his recounting of the Teaneck incident in his memoir.

Partiality may be a venial sin in an activist, but when Sharpton blamed the Howard Beach incident of 1986 on "the Reagan-Bush epoch," he bordered on deliberate misrepresentation. The incident involved a young black man named Michael Griffith who was chased out of a white neighborhood in Queens by a gang of local teenagers. Griffith fled onto a freeway where he was struck by a car and killed. Speaking of Howard Beach's white residents, Sharpton wrote in *Go and Tell Pharaoh*,

> Their rage came from years of white politicians, Nixon into Reagan on through Bush, telling white folks that the reason the country doesn't work is blacks. This led to the reenergizing of racism and race scapegoating. "Why are your taxes so high? Blacks. They're all on welfare and they're bankrupting us. Why is there so much unemployment in Howard Beach? Why can't the young people get meaningful work? Blacks."

As Sharpton well knew, New York's outer-borough ethnics did not get their resentments off the TV. Many of them had personally fled from nearby neighborhoods when crime and disorder exploded in the 1960s as Italian and Jewish residents were replaced by blacks and Puerto Ricans. The particular youths who chased Griffith out onto the Belt Parkway had been accosted by Griffith and his friends hours earlier. The three men had been jaywalking and almost ran into the teens' car. They banged on the hood, shouted, "Fuck you, honky," boasted that they were armed, and spat at the driver through the window. An autopsy also showed that Griffith had a "near-lethal level" of cocaine in his system. Three years earlier, Howard Beach had been targeted by a string of violent home invasions that netted tens of thousands of dollars from terrified elderly residents, one of whom nearly died of a heart attack. You could say many things about the dark psychological forces that surfaced that evening in 1986—that they were disproportionate, or primitive, or un-Christian—but not that they had been learned from Ronald Reagan.

Considering that it took place within the memory of people now living, it is strange that "white flight" has become such a lied-about subject. The quality of a civilization is judged by its great cities; for decades, beginning in the 1960s, ours were rendered uninhabitable. Yet today the official interpretation of that catastrophe is what James Baldwin said so glibly: "I do not bring down property values when I move in. You bring them down when you move out." Racism is the only cause of white flight that it is safe to mention. Ta-Nehisi Coates in his National Book Award–winning *Between the World and Me* spoke for the conventional wisdom when he blamed "self-generated fears that compelled the people who think they are white to flee the cities."

It was not "self-generated" fears that made the Jewish population of the Boston neighborhood of Mattapan fall from ten thousand to twenty-five hundred in the space of four years between 1968 and 1972. The neighborhood was experiencing as many as thirty robberies a week. With an influx of new black residents, street crime became epidemic. The local rabbi was temporarily blinded when acid was thrown in his face by two black youths who rang his doorbell and handed him a note telling him to "lead the Jewish racists out of Mattapan." Another rabbi repeatedly assured an elderly congregant that he would never abandon the neighborhood "as long as you are alive and come to the synagogue." The congregant was murdered in a break-in in 1973. "The elderly Jews live in fear for their lives and they are not wrong," a local dentist said. "I know because my office is in Dorchester and I have to repair their broken teeth."

Their black neighbors had not bought houses in Mattapan on their own dime. It was the government of Boston that put them there, in collaboration with local banks, as part of a $29 million program called Boston Banks Urban Renewal Group. Half of BBURG's subsidized homeowners would lose their houses to foreclosure or abandonment within five years; some never made a single payment on their loans. The consortium had deliberately selected a Jewish neighborhood as the venue for their experiment in residential integration, either because Jews were liberal and committed to making integration work (the benign explanation) or because they were politically weaker and less likely to riot than the Irish and Italians (what many Jews privately suspected). New York's city government played a similar role in ruining several Brooklyn and Queens neighborhoods, not just by building public housing there, but by refusing to screen public tenants for past drug convictions and violent crimes, for fear of getting hit with a civil liberties lawsuit.

Boris Kochubievsky was a Soviet dissident who served three years in a labor camp for attempting to immigrate to Israel. He visited Mattapan in May 1972 and was appalled by what he saw. "Even in the Soviet Union, Jews are not afraid to walk on the streets in their own neighborhoods after dark," he told his hosts. Among the

Jews displaced by street crime in New York City were many Holocaust survivors and refugees. One Canarsie grandmother made a comparison that rattled the sociologist who heard it: "I am locked up like in the ghettos of Europe. I am afraid of people knocking down my door. I still am not free."

How could this calamity be memory holed so thoroughly that, to the extent anyone remembers it today, we talk as if the Holocaust survivors were the villains of the story? It is because the boomers themselves were too young to remember it. Most people born in the decade after 1945 would have been in their twenties when Judge Garrity's busing decision came down, too old to be in school and too young to have children of their own.

Preserving the boomers' liberalism on race was, in many cases, precisely why their parents had fled to the suburbs. Bernie and Roz Ebstein of Chicago had marched with Martin Luther King and were committed to staying in Merrionette Manor even as the neighborhood flipped, until their school-age sons started expressing racial resentments. "You believe this stuff about integration," their eldest told them, "but we're living it." The Ebsteins quickly moved to Hyde Park, where little David and Steven would no longer have their liberal opinions beaten out of them. Having high-status views on race was part of the middle-class life they wanted to pass on to their children, no less than material comforts and a college education.

It is therefore a mark of white flight's success that so many boomers are willing to believe Ta-Nehisi Coates's lies about it. Coates has been one of the keenest enforcers of the new orthodoxy, blaming residential segregation and black neighborhood dysfunction on the (by now nearly century-old) bugbear of "redlining," not the violent traumas of the 1960s. But even Coates sometimes betrays the cognitive dissonance of his position.

In 2012, the McCarren Park Pool in Williamsburg, Brooklyn, was reopened after being closed thirty years earlier due to chronic violence and vandalism. On opening weekend, teens ended up causing a violent scuffle that led to the near drowning of a lifeguard, several injuries, and multiple arrests including for second-degree assault. The NYPD announced that a plainclothes team would be detailed to the pool going forward.

"Maybe I'm jaded but if I re-open a pool in New York, on a hot day, to much fanfare, I expect a crowd, I expect kids, and I expect beef," Coates wrote in a blog post about the brawl. "It is by no means shocking that some kids decided to rush a lifeguard instead of listening to him. You need cops there." It may surprise Coates to hear it, but there are many places in America where a day at the public pool is not a form of recreation thought to require a police presence. When a neighborhood changes from one kind to the other, residents have every right to consider it a change for the worse.

A natural consequence of our detachment from historical reality is that our racial discourse has become detached from *current* reality. University-trained radicals rail against microaggressions that their grandfathers would have struggled to discern. Pulpit rhetoric has been replaced by an arcane jargon devised by liberal arts professors. The boundaries of acceptable opinion shift at the whim of activists whose authority derives not from any following among actual people of color but from their meritocratic credentials or their social media savvy.

This was the roiling landscape that President Barack Obama put Al Sharpton in charge of managing for him.

It is sometimes forgotten that Obama did not launch onto the national scene enjoying unanimous support from the black community. Andrew Young endorsed Hillary Clinton in 2008 and joked that Bill Clinton "is every bit as black as Barack. He has probably gone out with more black women than Barack." The Congressional Black Caucus was split during the primary. Jesse Jackson endorsed Obama on March 30 but a few months later was caught on a hot mic during a Fox News appearance saying that he wanted "to cut [Obama's] nuts out" for "talking down to black people" in a Father's Day speech in which Obama talked about family breakdown. Jackson was effectively banned from the White House for the duration of Obama's two terms.

Sharpton, on the other hand, formed a bond with the candidate as early as the Iowa caucuses. Sharpton canceled a scheduled speech in Iowa at the last moment when Obama made it clear privately that a Sharpton appearance so close to the caucuses might hurt his chances with white voters there. Jesse Jackson had done a similar favor for Harold Washington when Obama was a young man in Chicago, lying low during his 1983 mayoral campaign. Then, on the night of Washington's election victory, Jackson seized the stage at the victory party and shouted, with news cameras rolling, "We won! We want it all!"—another reason Obama had for suspecting that Jesse was all about Jesse.

Sharpton consistently behaved himself throughout the 2008 campaign, and over time he earned the Obama camp's trust. With that trust came access. Sharpton visited the White House more than seventy times over Obama's two terms, which averages out to nearly a visit per month. He had visited the Clinton White House only twice. In exchange, Sharpton's job was to deal with race eruptions on the White House's behalf.

In some ways this was a reversion to the old Sharpton, not the svelte MSNBC host, but the tracksuited marcher. He coached the street peddler Eric Garner's family into extracting a $5.9 million settlement from the City of New York, even though a grand jury concluded that the fatal heart attack Garner suffered during his arrest had more to do with his being 350 pounds and asthmatic than any rough handling from the NYPD. He flew to Ferguson, Missouri, and addressed packed crowds during the week of rioting that followed the police shooting of Michael Brown. He disparaged the county prosecutor and called for a federal investigation into Brown's shooting, which he got, only to have the Justice Department report exonerate the officer. The important thing was that Sharpton was careful never to say anything that would embarrass the Obama administration, either by attacking them or by going off the reservation.

Sharpton's interventions spared Obama from having to weigh in on racial controversies himself, which was a relief to the White House. When the president tried, he usually gaffed—like when he said that if he'd had a son, he would look like Trayvon Martin, or when he said the Cambridge police had acted "stupidly" in arresting the Harvard professor Henry Louis Gates after he broke into his own home and then got belligerent with the cops who came to investigate reports of a burglary in progress. Both of these remarks prompted fierce backlash. It was better for the president to remain above it all. Sharpton therefore played a useful role.

It was not always easy for Sharpton to manage the younger radicals. The Black Lives Matter movement convinced many younger activists that they did not need leaders at all, just social media and people power. The generational conflict came to a head at a December 2014 march in Washington. The National Action Network had organized the march and thus felt entitled to restrict who could speak from its microphone. The younger protesters did not feel the same. "If it is a protest, why do you need to have a VIP pass?" asked one activist who had been denied permission to speak. DeRay Mckesson, the most visible Black Lives Matter organizer to come out of the Ferguson protests, tweeted, "I now have a problem with Sharpton."

But Sharpton had a trump card against the radicals, one Mayor Daley would have appreciated: he had actual support. Even his bitterest enemies have always admitted that about him. Ed Koch must have lost count of the number of times Sharpton called him a racist when he was mayor of New York, but even Koch conceded, "He is a bona fide black leader, and by leader I mean someone who can say, 'I need people to mobilize and to picket' and 5,000 people will come out." When Sharpton ran for mayor of New York City in 1997, he nearly forced the Manhattan borough president, Ruth Messinger, into a runoff, coming in second with 32 percent to her 39 percent in a city that was less than 30 percent black. When DeRay Mckesson ran for mayor of Baltimore in 2016, he got 2.6 percent—a grand total of 3,445 votes.

Dealing with radical race activists has been a problem for every post-boomer president. In 1963, John F. Kennedy had his brother Bobby ask James Baldwin to set up a meeting with black cultural leaders at the family apartment in New York. The meeting did not go well. A Freedom Rider named Jerome Smith told the president, a World War II veteran, that he felt no moral obligation to fight for his country. Things went downhill from there. Bobby vented to Arthur Schlesinger afterward, "They don't know what the laws are, they don't know what the facts are, they don't know what we've been doing or what we're trying to do. You can't talk to them the way you can talk to Martin Luther King or Roy Wilkins. . . . It was all emotion, hysteria."

Bobby, like his brother, was Honey Fitz's grandson. When he wondered why blacks didn't use the same methods the Irish had used to climb the social ladder, this was not bourgeois self-help boilerplate but the voice of personal and family experience. In the case of this particular meeting, it was not just that he grasped theoretically how blacks might use political organization to improve their condition. He was personally offering to use his position as attorney general and counselor to the president to assist them in doing so, which was more than the Boston Brahmins had ever done for his Irish ancestors.

James Baldwin, on the other hand, was a perfect example of someone whose political ideas were symbolic, which is to say that they were disconnected from reality. His writing thrills readers today with its categorical pronouncements: "To be a Negro in this country and to be relatively conscious is to be in a rage almost all the time." But these outbursts were not the hard-won lessons of a life spent under oppression. Quite the opposite. Baldwin was coddled by white America from the time he was in grade school. After being encouraged by Countee Cullen to apply, he was accepted to

DeWitt Clinton High School in the Bronx, where he was made editor of the literary magazine. Over his long career he won a Rosenwald fellowship, a Guggenheim Fellowship, a Saxton Award, a Ford Foundation grant, and a *Partisan Review* fellowship, to give only an abbreviated list. When he testified before a House committee in 1968, congressmen were positively fawning: "You have offered some very wonderful suggestions and some good comments." "We can't thank you enough for coming to see us. . . . We benefited enormously by your views."

Baldwin's writing was inspired not by oppression but by his personal neuroses, which, to be fair, anyone with his upbringing would have suffered from. He never knew his father. His abusive stepfather went insane and died when he was a teenager. He was sexually molested as a child by both men and women. He had a complex about being hideously ugly. Reading about his pathetic middle-aged affairs with unworthy gay lovers or the breakdowns that had him rolling on the floor of his New York apartment moaning, "I'm just so lonely," any human being would feel compassion for a man in so much pain. His error was to project his pain onto the black experience. He sneered at Richard Wright—who really did grow up in Mississippi and suffered more oppression firsthand than Baldwin ever heard of—for being shackled by racist complexes. But it was Baldwin who could not escape the traps in his own mind.

Arthur Schlesinger, the aide to whom Bobby Kennedy had vented after the disastrous meeting in 1963, had his own run-in with Baldwin many years later. Baldwin was one of several writers, including William Styron, Carlos Fuentes, and Arthur Miller, invited to attend François Mitterrand's inauguration in 1981. Baldwin asked for a plus-one. The French replied that none of the other writers' wives had been given tickets when they asked, but Baldwin insisted. Schlesinger's diary records the result: "They sent him two tickets on the Concorde. On arrival in Paris Jimmy and his current lover (male, of course) took off at once for the Côte d'Azur, spent the weekend in the sun, returned to Paris and took the Concorde back to New York, never going near Mitterrand and the inauguration."

Clearly for Baldwin being disconnected from reality did not mean he was unable to extract material benefits from white people. But Bobby Kennedy would have been baffled. Baldwin had once had the president and the attorney general in a room begging him to ask them for a favor, and he whiffed. Compared with that, what were a couple of comped plane tickets? Baldwin was opportunistic, but he had no systematic sense of how small favors could add up to real progress.

The rebellious Black Lives Matter activists are like Baldwin, always thinking transformationally and not transactionally in a way that, ironically, keeps them from seeing the big picture. In 2016, some BLM leaders even declined an invitation to meet with President Obama in the Oval Office, because they didn't want to be used for a photo op. Sharpton is savvier than that. If Bobby Kennedy had invited him to a meeting with JFK, he wouldn't have walked away empty-handed.

But does that mean he has found a happy balance between transformational and transactional leadership? Has he fused them in a useful combination, like when Adam Clayton Powell and Ray Jones worked together? Or is the mature boomer style of civil rights leadership, as exemplified by Sharpton, more like the worst of both worlds?

An interesting historical mystery is the question of who or what solved the sectarian problem in Ireland. For centuries Catholics and Protestants were at war, terrorist violence on one side, state oppression on the other. Even after the two were given separate countries to live in, the conflict persisted, a standing rebuke to the self-flattering notion that tribal conflicts were a Third World problem for primitive peoples. It was one of those intractable standing struggles like Israel-Palestine that the world's best diplomatic minds tackled again and again with no success. And then one day it dissolved into thin air. Suddenly the old murderous hatreds no longer seemed worth killing over.

What brought about this remarkable truce? It had little to do with the brotherhood of man. Religious hatreds started counting for less because religion counted for less. The Republic of Ireland was once a country where Catholics couldn't set foot in Protestant churches even for their best friend's funeral and Irish censors banned most of the books reviewed in *The Times Literary Supplement*. Then, gradually, contraception, divorce, abortion, and gay marriage were all legalized. Weekly Mass attendance dropped into the 30s, down from 85 percent as late as 1990. A third of Irish births are now out of wedlock. Even the most fanatical Ulster Presbyterian—of which there are also far fewer these days—no longer believes that rule by Dublin would be more distinctively Catholic than rule by Tony Blair. The Irish on both sides of the border have become fat, rich, and lazy like the rest of us. If this is victory, it is a sad kind of victory.

Some people anticipate that America's race problem will go the same way as Irish sectarianism. It may feel as if our racial tensions are intractable, burdened by centuries of suspicion and violence and bad faith. But millions of new Americans have no interest in the toxic dance between black and white. Their parents came from Asia and Latin America. All that gothic baggage means nothing to them. As America becomes not just biracial but truly multicultural, it is predicted that our original sin of racism will recede in importance.

Optimists about America's racial future point to other favorable signs, including, most obviously, the election of a black president. More black Americans than ever are middle-class. Black culture has become America's biggest cultural export. From Marseilles to Kinshasa to Seoul, rap is the universal language of youthful rebellion and swagger. It is extraordinary that young Englishmen in Devon, who might well have never met a black person in their lives, should believe that the height of cool consists in imitating the speech and dress of black Americans in Los Angeles in the early 1990s, but the chain-wearing, tracksuited chavs of Torquay suggest it is so. No longer does black culture have to struggle for respect. Thanks to globalization, it is culturally dominant on a scale never enjoyed even by Hollywood.

So there ought to be reason to hope that our national specter is ready to be exorcised. But the truth is that America's race problem is not gothic or ghost haunted. It survives not because we are psychologically too guilt-ridden to deal with it but because the people invested in it gain too much from it to let it go away. It is the most tawdry, boring thing in the world: group favoritism. It's patronage. These are not symptoms of Belfast-style blood hatreds but a rule of human behavior observable in every multiethnic society in history.

Conservatives have erred for decades in treating affirmative action as if it were self-evidently scandalous: *blacks and Latinos get admitted to UC Berkeley with scores in the 34th percentile, while whites and Asians get rejected with scores in the 99th!* By the standards of equality under the law, that is indeed an outrage. But by the standards of human history, it is tediously ordinary. It is no more than Tammany Hall did when it made sure its election slate (mayor, city council president, comptroller) was always a balanced ticket: one Irish, one Italian, one Jewish/other. Groups compete for resources, and keeping the peace between them requires monitoring how resources are apportioned. New Yorkers cared about the ethnic division of power, so Tammany did, too.

The problem today is not that we have regressed to the old machine politics. It is that we have all of the old machine politicians' vices and none of their virtues. The D.C. mayor Marion Barry was quite a step down from the old Irish bosses. At one point he had nearly one in thirteen D.C. residents on the municipal payroll; Boss Tweed would have been appalled at the inefficiency. He would also have been appalled at the sanctimony. Barry cloaked his most brazen peculations in the high-flown language of civil rights, even after he was busted smoking crack on FBI surveillance video. In the eyes of his supporters, standing up to the white power structure justified any level of corruption and waste in the actual operations of the city government—far more corruption and waste than Tammany's voters would have stood for. Tammany rule was always punctuated by intervals of reform when voters got fed up, whereas Marion Barry held office in D.C. pretty much continuously until his death, except for the brief period when he was actually incarcerated.

Marion Barry is a particularly crude example of the way we disguise raw racial patronage with pretty lies, but are the pretty lies of the University of California admissions office so different? The UC system claims (and the California Civil Rights Initiative passed by referendum in 1996 legally requires) that it does not use race as a factor in admissions. But it achieves the same outcome by adjusting in race-conscious ways the kinds of merit it recognizes. Our legal system is able to reconcile affirmative action with the Civil Rights Act only by pretending that *preferences* are fundamentally different from *quotas*, even when preferences yield suspiciously quota-like stability to a school's racial balance. America is not willing to accept a world where Harvard is less than 1 percent black, but neither are we willing to admit that Harvard admissions should be determined by what is politically acceptable, so the school justifies its affirmative action program in the language of diversity and justice.

Obviously the immigrants in whom America's race-relations optimists place their hopes have no interest in preserving the political power of the likes of Marion Barry. But they are happy to uphold the structures that benefit African Americans, because they benefit from them, too. Affirmative action means Hispanic kids get into better schools than they deserve and pay less for the privilege. Indian entrepreneurs benefit from racially targeted loans from the Small Business Administration. Complaining about underrepresentation of Asians in media means better distribution deals for movies like *Crazy Rich Asians*.

If we were able to discuss these patronage programs rationally, we would see that they make no sense. Why target small business loans to Indians, who have a higher average income and education than whites, especially when the program was originally intended to help disadvantaged blacks? Why should immigrants be favored over natives by affirmative action programs from the moment their feet hit the tarmac? Why are programs intended to compensate for past discrimination available to people who just got here and who came to America voluntarily? The answer to all of these questions is, Who cares? These programs are needed to sustain the Democratic coalition. In California, that coalition has already grown into a permanent one-party majority, and the rest of America may follow, depending on demographic trends.

The boomers opted for transformational leadership, but the transactional keeps coming back. They tried to depoliticize racial issues as much as possible, by placing them beyond the reach of the democratic process and in the hands of judges and bureaucrats, but at the same time they created a multiethnic America where the task of balancing group interests is more necessary than ever. That does not mean that Al Sharpton is the kind of leader we need. But he does something that needs doing, which means that if we don't come up with a better substitute, he is the kind of leader we will be stuck with—along with the increasingly unaccountable judges.

7

SONIA SOTOMAYOR

The conservative bloc on the Supreme Court was ready to issue a ruling in *Fisher v. University of Texas* (2013) that would have limited the use of race in college admissions, when Justice Sonia Sotomayor persuaded Anthony Kennedy to change his vote. It was not the cogency of her arguments that persuaded him. Kennedy had been a reliable vote against affirmative action throughout his twenty-five years on the bench, going back to *Metro Broadcasting v. FCC* in 1990 and as recently as *Grutter v. Bollinger* in 2003, when he dissented from Sandra Day O'Connor's opinion upholding affirmative action as long as race is only one narrowly tailored factor out of many. But sometime between oral argument on October 10, 2012, and the announcement of the opinion on June 24, 2013, Sotomayor circulated a blistering draft dissent that made Kennedy change his mind.

That draft dissent has never been published, but when the veteran Supreme Court reporter Joan Biskupic started asking around about what had happened with *Fisher*, which Court watchers noticed was not announced until the last week of the term, months after the other cases argued in October had been decided, she heard from insiders that "I would soon see a version of it." Apparently the text of that draft was repurposed for Sotomayor's dissent in *Schuette v. Coalition to Defend Affirmative Action* (2014), which upheld a Michigan state constitutional amendment banning racial preferences. Justices don't always read their dissenting opinions aloud from the bench when decisions are announced, but in *Schuette*, for the first time, Sotomayor read hers.

Her dissent begins with an introduction comparing the voters of Michigan to the white majority that imposed Jim Crow, a comparison that Justice Antonin Scalia, in his concurring opinion, calls "shameful." It crescendos to a deeply personal explanation of why her colleagues' hopes for a color-blind solution to racial inequality are "out of touch with reality," introducing the boomer vocabulary of therapy and trauma into the normally arid language of judicial opinion:

> Race matters for reasons that really are only skin deep, that cannot be discussed any other way, and that cannot be wished away. Race matters to a young man's view of society when he spends his teenage years watching others tense up as he passes, no matter the neighborhood where he grew up. Race matters to a young woman's sense of self when she states her hometown, and then is pressed, "No, where are you really from?" regardless of how many generations her family has been in the country. Race matters to a young person addressed by a stranger in a foreign language, which he does not understand because only English

was spoken at home. Race matters because of the slights, the snickers, the silent judgments that reinforce that most crippling of thoughts: "I do not belong here."

Some justices on the current Court respond badly to emotional blackmail. Chief Justice John Roberts was so incensed that he wrote his own two-paragraph concurrence entirely devoted to criticizing Sotomayor for attacking the majority in such personal terms ("People can disagree in good faith on this issue, but [it] does more harm than good to question the openness and candor of those on either side of the debate"). Scalia, as we saw, thought such histrionics disgraceful. But on Kennedy—the man who loved to be hailed as the conscience of the Court, who pondered tough questions by walking back and forth across his office courtyard in the pose of Rodin's *Thinker*, the man to whom wags applied the term "the Greenhouse Effect," after the *New York Times* correspondent Linda Greenhouse, whose approval Kennedy craved—on Kennedy, it worked.

Those "slights" and "snickers" that say "I do not belong here" are a staple of Sotomayor's public persona. Her memoir, for which she received a reported $1.175 million advance, is full of references to her insecurities. At lectures in front of middle schoolers, on *The Daily Show*, on *The View* (where the ladies addressed her as "Sonia"), Sotomayor reassures her audiences that even with all her accomplishments she still hears a voice in her head asking, "Am I really here? Do I really belong?" Like many boomers, Sotomayor has shaped her persona around a psychological narrative of personal growth, from self-doubt to self-acceptance.

When she was nominated as President Barack Obama's first Supreme Court appointee, it was hoped that Sotomayor could become "the people's justice." Her biography was certainly compelling: growing up poor in the Bronx, diagnosed with diabetes when she was seven, alcoholic father dead when she was nine, raised thereafter by her nurse single mother and loving *abuelita*. There was some controversy during her confirmation over a speech in which Sotomayor expressed hope that a "wise Latina woman, with the richness of her experiences, would more often than not reach a better conclusion than a white male who hasn't lived that life." Her defenders responded that the "wise Latina" quote was merely arguing for judges to draw on the richness of their diverse backgrounds. In her *Schuette* dissent, however, Justice Sotomayor showcased not the richness of her Latina background but only its resentments.

Hard as it may be for her to believe, Sotomayor is not the first Supreme Court justice to feel out of place. Charles E. Whittaker was the second justice appointed by Eisenhower, after Earl Warren, and his short tenure was blighted by his feelings of inferiority. He was not Hispanic, or female, or even Jewish. He was a straight white Protestant male from Kansas. But he had dropped out of high school at sixteen and gone to an unaccredited night school for his law degree, and colleagues like Felix Frankfurter and William O. Douglas intimidated him. "You know Charlie had gone to night law school, and he began as an office boy and he'd been a farm boy, and he had inside him an inferiority complex," one justice told Earl Warren's biographer. "He used to come out of our conferences literally crying . . . he'd say, 'Felix used words in there I had never heard of.'" Eventually Whittaker had a nervous breakdown and resigned in 1962.

Coming from humble beginnings does not determine how someone will end up. Everything depends on how a person handles it.

Harry Truman attended the same unaccredited Kansas City night school as Whittaker, before poverty forced him to drop out, and Truman turned out fine. A disadvantaged background made Charlie Whittaker a neurotic. It made Sonia Sotomayor a bully. The boomers' preoccupation with oppression, identity, and grievance would create many bullies, because it turns out that thinking of yourself as a victim can make you heedless of the ways your actions victimize others.

Sotomayor learned early in life that something about her gave her the power to make authority figures hop. As a sophomore at Princeton, she and other members of the activist group Acción Puertorriqueña sent a formal letter of complaint to the federal Department of Health, Education, and Welfare accusing Princeton of not hiring enough Hispanics. "The facts imply and reflect the total absence of regard, concern and respect for an entire people and their culture," she explained to *The Daily Princetonian* in May 1974. "In effect, they reflect an attempt—a successful attempt so far—to relegate an important cultural sector of the population to oblivion." Within weeks, HEW sent a federal official to New Jersey to meet with Sotomayor and an associate provost, who agreed to send Sotomayor an official minority hiring plan by the end of June.

Looking back on those years in her memoir, Sotomayor describes her undergraduate experience as a struggle to fit in, but in activism she found a psychological reinforcement more potent than belonging: power. The tone of her letter was hardly ingratiating. By pre-boomer standards, it was abusive. But far from urging this intemperate full-ride scholarship student that she should make more of an effort to fit in, Princeton quickly hired a Latino assistant dean of students who was on campus in time to greet Sotomayor when she returned for her junior year in September.

Her complaint to HEW was not, strictly speaking, a protest. The officials who received it welcomed its message. So did Princeton. The minority hiring plan "would have been prepared and submitted whether or not there had been a student complaint," an administrator admitted later. Shortly before Sotomayor sent her letter, the board of trustees had voted $200,000 to refurbish the Third World Center, the campus hub for minority student groups, including Acción Puertorriqueña. The university was not only willing but eager to meet activists' demands. Any posture of protest on the students' part was mere playacting.

Sotomayor encountered more resistance when she tried the same gambit at Yale Law School. At a recruiting dinner for law students in 1978, a partner from the firm Shaw, Pittman grilled her about affirmative action: "Do you think you would have been admitted to Yale Law School if you were not Puerto Rican? . . . Do law firms do a disservice by hiring minority students who they know do not have the necessary credentials and will then fire in three to four years? . . . Do you consider yourself culturally deprived?" No doubt he was testing her to see how she would react. When Antonin Scalia had a similar dinner with prospective employers at the Cleveland-based law firm Jones, Day shortly after graduating from Harvard Law, the partners hammered the devout Catholic on blue laws mandating Sunday shop closings, which Scalia was the only one at the table to support. "They really put it to him," one of his hosts remembered, "and he handled it beautifully."

Sotomayor did not accept her interrogation in a similar spirit.

She filed an official complaint accusing Shaw, Pittman of violating Yale's antidiscrimination policy and questioning their right to recruit on campus in the future. A faculty-student tribunal found in Sotomayor's favor and demanded a letter of apology, which Shaw, Pittman sent and then redrafted in more abject terms when their first letter of apology was deemed inadequate by Yale officials. Funnily enough, when Sotomayor showed up for her one-on-one interview the day after the disastrous group dinner, the partner who had grilled her invited her to come to Washington for more interviews. He thought she had handled the questioning well.

The journey from Bronx housing project to Ivy League law school had taught Sotomayor resilience. But it also taught her that bullying would yield results, that she would never pay a price for acting out; on the contrary, that she would be rewarded. This was, in a way, an appropriate lesson for her to learn. She was about to enter a profession that made a decades-long mission of bullying America.

The United States has been known as a land of lawyers since the eighteenth century. Edmund Burke and Alexis de Tocqueville both remarked on it. But it was not until the boomer era that the profession really came into its own, thanks in part to the rise of public interest law, the legal equivalent of an industrial revolution.

In the first half of the twentieth century, a nonprofit with a name like the German Legal Aid Society could be assumed to provide pro bono legal work for indigent clients from the demographic group named in its title. The Mexican American Legal Defense and Educational Fund, founded in 1968, was more interested in *changing* the law, winning cases that would set far-reaching precedents. Eventually, many of the big public interest law firms stopped accepting routine cases lacking landmark potential. The purpose of public interest law at that point was to take the liberal eruptions of the Warren Court, which had caught the country by surprise, and make them routine. There were fifty full-time public interest lawyers in the country when Chief Justice Warren resigned in 1969. By 1975, there were six hundred.

Many of the great Warren Court cases were brought by independent individuals like Clarence Earl Gideon and Ernesto Miranda, whose cases were taken up by groups like the ACLU late in the process, if at all. The precedent-setting cases after 1970 were more likely to have been conceived, designed, and executed by nonprofit law firms from the very beginning. *Serrano v. Priest*, which forced California to equalize school funding across the state because allowing rich counties to spend more on education than poor counties violated the Fourteenth Amendment, was the brainchild of the (federally funded) Western Center on Law and Poverty. The Puerto Rican Legal Defense and Education Fund, on whose board Sonia Sotomayor served from 1980 to 1992, launched and won cases forcing New York to offer bilingual education in public schools, redraw city council districts, and print government forms in Spanish, all without going to the trouble of winning an election.

The industrial manufacture of left-wing precedents was not the practice of law as it had been known for centuries. Common-law offenses like barratry and maintenance had to be thrown out the window. The purpose of those antique torts had been to prevent third parties from subsidizing legal action for purposes of their own, using the client as a cat's-paw. Subsidizing legal action for purposes of your own, independent of your client's, is what public interest law *is*. Traditionally, attorneys are not allowed to solicit clients but must wait for clients to come to them. This, too, is to ensure that cases are brought only by clients who are personally invested in the outcome and whose self-interest can be appealed to in reaching a reasonable settlement.

The Equal Employment Opportunity Commission, by contrast, used to send its lawyers around the country in the 1970s canvassing for plaintiffs who had been discriminated against at work. When the EEOC decided to go after a particular employer, it would put ads in the local paper inviting former employees to come and testify (and, of course, collect their share of the payout if the case was successful). The Supreme Court ruled in the 1978 case *In re Primus* that a lawyer for the ACLU was permitted to solicit clients by mail, contrary to bar regulations, because she did it for a political cause and not for her own profit. By the time the gay rights movement hit its stride at the turn of the century, no one any longer thought it odd that such far-reaching social changes should be accomplished through highly choreographed plaintiff selection and organized harassment of shop owners. The old Brandeisian notion that cases must involve an "earnest and vital controversy" arising naturally from the frictions of society was dead.

The EEOC also pioneered the contagious new tactic of proving guilt by statistics. The earlier Progressives had been hailed as revolutionaries for introducing statistics into the legal process through their sociological briefs, but the EEOC did them one better. The Progressives used social science to demonstrate why women should not work thirteen-hour shifts in canning factories, but in order to convict a cannery owner for violating the law, you still needed an actual woman with an actual time card. Under civil rights laws, guilt could be proved based on statistical disparities alone. An EEOC case filed in 1973 against Sears went on for twelve years at a cost of millions of dollars, yet the trial featured not a single woman who claimed to have been discriminated against. The government's case was entirely statistical.

As judges came to decide more matters that had previously been left to elected politicians, the judicial process came to resemble politics in all its rowdiness. More than 500,000 pro-choice protesters descended on Washington in advance of the oral argument in *Planned Parenthood v. Casey* in 1992. This demonstration would have been recognized as inappropriate in an era when judicial impartiality was still taken seriously. If judges merely apply the law, it should not matter what half a million demonstrators think. But the protesters' show of force was rewarded. When the *Casey* decision came down, it explicitly grounded its refusal to overturn *Roe* in the need to protect "the people's acceptance of the judiciary."

The circus quality of modern Supreme Court nominations is a direct result of this politicization. Like public interest law, this spectacle is something genuinely new. For most of the Supreme Court's history, nominees did not even attend their own hearings. The Left is to blame for the current state of affairs, and not just because it was Democrats who fired the first shot against Robert Bork in 1987 and launched the war of escalation that has led to the current standoff. Empowering the judiciary to meddle deeper in politics in the name of constantly evolving constitutional rights is what has made the stakes of each nomination so high. The people who talk in lofty terms about the exalted role of judges in our democracy are the ones responsible for forcing the nomination process down in the muck.

Sotomayor did not enjoy her confirmation process. A White House "war room" is a grueling experience for any nominee, and Sotomayor did not approach hers in an obliging frame of mind. "There were private questions I was offended by," she complained later. "I wondered if they ever asked those questions of the male candidates. But the society has a double standard." In fact, Anthony Kennedy remembers being asked by White House lawyers when he first had sex and if he'd ever had an STD or dabbled in S&M, among other intrusive questions, and that was before the advent of twenty-four-hour cable news when scrutiny of hearings was less intense. White House staffers also told Jeffrey Toobin of *The New Yorker* that Sotomayor resented being forced to prepare detailed answers on "the full range of constitutional law," making her sessions "tense and laborious."

To be fair to Sotomayor, she had a rougher confirmation than most. Her critics did not hesitate to criticize her in the most demeaning terms. "Bluntly put, she's not nearly as smart as she seems to think she is," Laurence Tribe told President Obama in a confidential memo that was later leaked. He wanted his Harvard Law dean, Elena Kagan, nominated instead, not just because she was smarter, but because she would have a better chance of persuading Anthony Kennedy to side with the liberals in cases where he was a swing vote. With Sotomayor, "her reputation for being something of a bully could well make her liberal impulses backfire and simply add to the fire power of the Roberts/Alito/Scalia/Thomas wing."

Even more humiliating was Jeffrey Rosen's hit piece in *The New Republic*, "The Case Against Sotomayor," which again hammered her supposed intellectual shortcomings. Anonymous quotations from clerks who worked with Sotomayor on the Second Circuit Court of Appeals piled insult on insult. "Not that smart and kind of a bully on the bench," said one. "She has an inflated opinion of herself, and is domineering during oral arguments but her questions aren't penetrating and don't get to the heart of the issue," said another. Rosen's idea of giving a balanced view was to quote a third clerk as saying, "She's a fine Second Circuit judge. Maybe not the smartest ever, but how often are Supreme Court nominees the smartest ever?"

The irony was that Tribe and Rosen had both defended affirmative action in the past. It probably did not occur to Professor Tribe when he was defending the *Bakke* decision in a public debate with Alan Dershowitz in 1977 that the principles he was propounding ("Lower scores and grades need not mean lower ability") would come back to bite him. He probably believed that for the really important stuff, like Supreme Court nominations, affirmative action would yield to pure meritocracy. Lucky for him, he did not accurately predict what forms of persuasion would work best on Anthony Kennedy.

It annoyed Sotomayor to read these attacks on her competence, especially from anonymous sources and especially from writers on her own political side. She blamed racism: "People kept accusing me of not being smart enough. Now, could someone explain to me, other than that I'm Hispanic, why that would be?" If attaining the summit of her profession put Sotomayor in a reflective mood, she might have cast her mind back on the Shaw, Pittman partner thirty years earlier who tried to get her to think through some of the unintended consequences of affirmative action, how it can rebound on its supposed beneficiaries and affect the way they are perceived. This was exactly the kind of thing he was talking about.

It should not have mattered so much to Tribe and Rosen whether Sotomayor was the smartest candidate on offer. Earl Warren was as dumb as a post, and he changed America more than any single human being in the second half of the twentieth century.

Warren truly was lackluster in the brains department. Felix Frankfurter referred to him privately as "that dumb Swede." During Thurgood Marshall's confirmation hearing in 1967, a Senate staffer's private memo stated in the nominee's favor that "he is not as dumb as Warren." Euphemisms like "relatively small capacity for verbal analysis" (Learned Hand) could not disguise the lack of esteem for the chief justice's intellect in the legal community. Often colleagues would debate a subtle legal point with the chief justice, only to run up against the hard thud of a prejudice like, in the 1969 flag-burning case *Street v. New York*, "It's the American flag. I'm just not going to vote in favor of burning the American flag."

In a way, being dumb was Warren's superpower. He was able to demolish long-standing precedents by pretending not to understand the reasoning behind them. The 1968 case *Levy v. Louisiana* overturned centuries of law by declaring that distinguishing between legitimate and illegitimate children amounted to "invidious discrimination" with no rational basis. A moment's thought might have revealed the rational basis behind the fact that every language in human history has had a term for bastard. By refusing to grasp the elementary logic of incentives, the justices were able to give their humanitarian sentiments free rein, at the cost of one of the oldest pillars of family law.

The decisions of the Warren Court reshaped America dramatically. *New York Times v. Sullivan* is the reason that, by the standards of other Western countries, it is practically impossible to win a libel action in the United States. Clearance rates on violent crimes took a nosedive after *Miranda*. The first draft of the majority opinion in *Griswold v. Connecticut* struck down contraceptive bans as a violation of freedom of association, but Justice William O. Douglas was mocked so mercilessly by Hugo Black for his draft opinion ("The right of the husband and wife to assemble in bed is a new right of assembly for me," Black chuckled) that Douglas took William Brennan's suggestion and based the decision on a right to privacy instead. Of course, he had to invent that right practically from whole cloth, but that was a small price to pay for enabling the sexual revolution.

Of all the realms of life affected by the Warren Court, none was harmed more, with less reason, than religion.

If you wanted to eradicate religion from a country, how would you go about it? The Soviets gave much thought to this question. You can't oppress it out of existence. As the enlightenment commissar Anatoly Lunacharsky said, "Religion is like a nail. The harder you hit it, the deeper it goes into the wood." What the Russians did instead was to ban religious instruction of the young. This had the advantage of being nominally consistent with liberal values of free exercise (which the Soviets professed to believe in) but, in practical terms, was devastating. No religion on earth can sustain itself without being passed along to children, and children who are never taught the habits of piety will find it difficult to develop them when they are older. Religion is like a language. Teach someone a language when he is young, and when he grows up, he can learn another. Teach him no language, and he will be a wolf boy forever.

In the United States, the watershed case was *Abington School District v. Schempp* in 1963. Over the previous fifteen years, the Supreme Court had built up an inconsistent wall of separation between education and religion. Released time for religious instruction was okay (*Zorach v. Clauson*, 1952) as long as it didn't take place on public school property (*McCollum v. Board of Education*, 1948); states could devote public funds to parochial school buses (*Everson v. School Board*, 1947) and textbooks (*Cochran v. Louisiana State Board of Education*, 1930) but not the schools themselves. *Engel v. Vitale* in 1962 was the first ruling to forbid school prayer—specifically a twenty-two-word voluntary, nondenominational prayer drafted by the New York legislature—but that struck down a practice that existed in one state, in only 10 percent of its schools. *Schempp* struck down two practices that were in use in half the schools in the country: Bible reading and the Lord's Prayer.

The star of the case was not the title family, unprepossessing Philadelphia Unitarians plucked from obscurity only because the ACLU was desperate for a school prayer case with a non-Jewish plaintiff, but rather Madalyn Murray O'Hair, a fire-breathing Baltimore atheist whose case the Supreme Court consolidated with the Schempps'. The ACLU kept Murray at arm's length because it sensed she was bad news. She had applied for Russian citizenship in 1959, so enamored was she of the Soviet system, and only dropped her application when a member of the American Communist Party told her that she would be more use to the cause where she was. She was also personally unpleasant, as the rest of America had ample cause to learn during her subsequent years of celebrity as the loud-mouthed president of American Atheists. "Compared to most cud-chewing, small-talking stupid American women, I'm a brain," she told *Life* magazine in 1964. "We might as well admit it, I'm a genius."

When Murray marched into Woodbourne Junior High to pro-test the voluntary recitation of the Lord's Prayer in her son's class, a school counselor told her, "There were prayers in the schools of this city before there was a United States of America. If our forefathers had wanted us to stop this practice, they would have told us that when they formed the government." Today when we think of excep-tions to strict separationism that have been grandfathered in be-cause the practice is so old, we think of military chaplains and invocation prayers at city council meetings. They obviously violate the establishment clause just as much as a Nativity scene in the city hall lobby, but they seem so venerable that it would be an act of hostility to abolish them. But prayer in American schools is more ancient than either of those practices, and much more important to society. "The exercise of public worship appears to be the only solid foundation of the religious sentiments of the people, which derive their force from imitation and habit," wrote Gibbon in a passage explaining the relatively peaceful method by which the emperor Theodosius brought an end to paganism. "The interruption of that public exercise may consummate, in the period of a few years, the important work of a national revolution."

If the change was so revolutionary, why was there no revolt against it, aside from a constitutional amendment that did not even pass the House? The answer can be found in a short book, *Prayer in the Public Schools: Law and Attitude Change* by William K.

Muir Jr., a political scientist at Berkeley. Muir happened to be studying a suburban school district he called Midland in 1963 and so was able to interview subjects before and after the *Schempp* decision came down on June 17. Among supporters of school prayer, the most common reaction Muir found was not protest, or acquiescence, but conversion. The principal who in the spring told him, "Morals have got to have a religious basis," in the fall said, "Morals do not boil down to one thing, they boil down to a combination of things." The black social worker who previously told him that prayer means so "much [when] you're in trouble" now said that kids "don't get anything out of" school prayer anyway. It was not that their previous opinions were insincere. More likely they convinced themselves that what was happening was all right because the alternative—accepting that a pudgy self-involved Communist had almost single-handedly eliminated a practice older than the country whose Constitution she so brazenly manipulated—would have been psychologically too much to bear.

It took multiple generations, but the elimination of every trace of religion from public schools has had its enervating effect. It is not necessarily cause for alarm that so few millennials belong to an organized church. There is a natural ebb and flow to religiosity over the life cycle, and most millennials are still in the relatively unchurched phase that precedes having kids of their own. What is alarming is that only 29 percent of millennials report attending weekly services as children, and nearly a fifth say that they were raised in no religion at all. Only 5 percent of boomers said the same.

The thing about traditional institutions like church is that we go most of our lives without needing them, but when we do need them, we need them very much. The boomers at least had firsthand experience with the churches they later rebelled against, which gave them religious instincts that they could revive in times of need. Millennials unchurched from the beginning will discover, in their moments of crisis when they need religion very much, that they have nothing to fall back on.

By the time Sonia Sotomayor was sworn in on August 8, 2009, having a woman on the Supreme Court was no big deal. Sandra Day O'Connor had been appointed almost thirty years earlier. In 2016, law schools became more than 50 percent female in their enrollment, and they have remained majority female ever since. More broadly, the expanded importance of law in American life since the 1960s made women more powerful, sometimes in unexpected ways. The professions called into existence by the rights revolution—the personnel managers and human resources directors who hardly existed in 1960 but who are now indispensable to making sure employers don't unlawfully discriminate on the basis of sex or race or disability—run female at rates of up to 75 percent.

It was an open question in the early days of feminism whether women were going to assimilate into previously male spaces by adopting masculine ways or transform them and make them more feminine. When she arrived on the Supreme Court, Sotomayor was not interested in assimilating into anything.

Some first-year justices lie low out of deference to the more senior justices. Not Sotomayor, whose interruptions—not just of lawyers, but of other justices in the middle of asking their own questions—are so frequent that Chief Justice Roberts sometimes has to reprimand her or give an attorney extra time to finish his remarks. During oral argument for *Department of Commerce v. New York*, on whether the 2020 census could ask respondents their citizenship status, Sotomayor interrupted the solicitor general fifty-eight times in eighty minutes, a record number of interruptions for any justice that term. In 2013 she was so quick to seize the floor that she managed to talk over the famously taciturn Clarence Thomas's only intervention in a decade.

Every year, at the end of the term, the outgoing clerks put on a comedy revue for the justices, with satirical skits and musical parodies. No spouses or outsiders are invited. The first time Sotomayor attended this annual party, in June 2010, she stood up when the clerks were finished and told them their skits "lacked a certain something." Salsa music started playing, and she got up and started dancing—a breach of protocol as the justices themselves never take part in the show. She then pressured the other justices to get up and dance with her, even Ruth Bader Ginsburg, whose beloved husband, Marty, had died just three days earlier. According to the reporter Joan Biskupic, Sotomayor told Ginsburg that her dead husband would have wanted her to dance. Biskupic's overall verdict on the other justices' reaction to Sotomayor disruptive performance, based on what her informants told her, was this: "I cannot tell you how uncomfortable many of them were."

The first American to actively sabotage the pomp of the Supreme Court was Thomas Jefferson, who made sure that justices on the bench did not wear wigs ("the monstrous wig which makes the English judges look like rats peeping through bunches of oakum!"). He would have preferred they didn't wear robes, either, but Hamilton won that one. Jefferson's hostility to the trappings of dignity was connected to his being the most Jacobin of the Founding Fathers. His aesthetic judgments had ideological correlates. The same is true of other liberals. When Sotomayor crassly asked if she could swear in Vice President Joe Biden a day early in 2013 because she had a book talk at a Barnes & Noble promoting her memoir scheduled for Inauguration Day, that was a lapse of decorum. But the same cavalier attitude is a running theme in liberal jurisprudence, on matters more important than vice presidential scheduling.

The great Warren Court radical William Brennan used to waggle his fingers at his colleagues and say, with stomach-turning smugness, "Five votes can do anything around here." But even liberal justices who don't feel particularly bound by the text of the Constitution are still constrained by their own sense of what they can get away with. Why did nineteen years elapse between Justice Kennedy's opinion in *Romer v. Evans*, decreeing a constitutional right for gays to have sex, and *Obergefell v. Hodges*, decreeing their right to marry? *Obergefell* explicitly denied that its finding was based on evolving social norms. "It is of no moment whether advocates of same-sex marriage now enjoy or lack momentum in the democratic process," Kennedy insisted. Their right derived not from society but from the Fourteenth Amendment. The reason this right had not been discerned earlier was simply the assessment of the liberal justices, and the activists who arranged their test cases, of what the country would stand for.

Someone's sense of what they can get away with also depends on their feeling for institutional norms, their sense of themselves as guardians of a tradition that existed before them and will continue after them. Even finger-waggling Brennan could not bring himself to think of the Court merely as his own personal plaything. But as concern for the traditions of the Court diminishes, even in regard to small matters like external courtesies, this sense of institutional guardianship diminishes, too.

In *Trump v. Hawaii* (2018), a narrow majority upheld a presidential proclamation restricting entry into the United States from a handful of predominantly Muslim countries, a travel restriction known popularly, but inaccurately, as a Muslim ban. Justice Sotomayor's dissent in that case cites President Trump multiple times by name and accuses him of issuing the proclamation out of "anti-Muslim animus" that "masquerades behind a façade of national-security concerns." Traditionally, Supreme Court opinions do not refer to politicians by name, as a matter of decorum—especially not in the sneering way Sotomayor does Trump. The substance of her argument, too, refuses to accord the president the deference to which he is customarily entitled.

The "animus" doctrine says that a government action can be invalidated if it is found to be based on "a bare desire to harm a politically unpopular group." It has been used to strike down changes to welfare qualifications for nonfamilial households (for animus against hippies and their unconventional living arrangements), zoning permit denials for group homes (for animus against the mentally handicapped), and an Arizona law banning the teaching in state schools of various grievance-driven disciplines like Chicano studies (for animus toward minorities). It is used sparingly, perhaps because judges sense that once they begin striking down state actions because politicians are mean, there can be no logical end to it. In *Trump v. Hawaii*, Sotomayor used this doctrine to argue that the executive order was unconstitutional because motivated by anti-Muslim animus. She cited in support of this various stump speeches from the campaign as well as a Fox News appearance by Rudy

Giuliani that appeared to provide a crucial link between the executive order, which the solicitor general emphatically denied was directed at Muslims, and the phrase "Muslim ban."

Would her judgment have been different if Giuliani had skipped Fox News that day? It is doubtful. The overall thrust of her opinion is that Trump is a bad man. Judicial activism used to mean judges striking down laws not because they were unconstitutional, but because they were unwise in the judge's opinion, which was overreaching enough. Now we have judges striking down laws, not because they don't like them, but because they don't like the politicians who enacted them. The Warren Court opened the door to unlimited judicial activism, but it took a younger, bolder generation to shed the self-imposed limits on arbitrary power that the pre-boomer generations still felt.

Since the eighteenth century, the British constitutional doctrine of parliamentary supremacy has traditionally been explained by the maxim, "Parliament can do anything except make a man into a woman or a woman into a man." Two and a half centuries after the philosopher Jean-Louis de Lolme came up with that line, Judge James Tayler ruled that the tax specialist Maya Forstater had no claim against her employer after she was fired for expressing her belief that sex is a matter of biology and trans women are biologically men. According to the judgment, Forstater's beliefs are "incompatible with human dignity" and "not worthy of respect in a democratic society." Parliament may not be able make a man into a woman, but today Judge Tayler can.

On the subject of transgender rights, Sotomayor joined the majority in the 2020 cases *Bostock v. Clayton County* and *Harris Funeral Homes v. EEOC*, which extended the antidiscrimination protections of Title VII of the Civil Rights Act of 1964 to the gay and transgendered. The Supreme Court concluded that the 1964 Congress that passed the CRA intended—or, if it did not intend, should reasonably have foreseen—that banning discrimination against women would also mean permitting individuals to shuttle between the sexes at will, an assertion only slightly less implausible than Judge Tayler's. In 1964, sodomy was illegal in forty-nine states; the concept of transgenderism barely existed.

In her *Schuette* dissent, Sotomayor urged white Americans to discuss discrimination with greater candor. "The way to stop discrimination on the basis of race is to speak openly and candidly on the subject of race," she writes. "We ought not sit back and wish away, rather than confront, the racial inequality that exists in our society." But is this invitation sincere, or is it a booby trap? Candor didn't much help Maya Forstater or the proprietors of Harris Funeral Homes when civil rights law decided that their opinions were out of bounds.

Nor did it help Larry Summers, who was forced to resign as president of Harvard after remarks he made at a conference on diversity in science and engineering in 2005. Summers hypothesized that the underrepresentation of women at the highest levels of the hard sciences might be due to differences in aptitudes and interests between the sexes similar to long-attested and objectively measurable disparities in things like "height, weight, propensity to criminality." The speech was supposed to be off the record, but a concerted campaign by feminists prompted a media firestorm and forced Summers to publish a verbatim transcript of what had been extemporaneous remarks. The Faculty of Arts and Sciences passed a vote of no confidence in Summers's leadership, after which he decided to resign.

Even those who think Summers should have kept his job tend to view it as a cultural and not a First Amendment issue because it was the free choice of the faculty and the board and, ultimately, Summers himself. But it must have occurred to the bright minds in Cambridge that Summers's remarks opened the university up to *legal* liability. A few years earlier, an English professor had sued Boston University for gender discrimination after she was denied tenure, and her case partly relied on remarks made by the university's president in a speech at a Washington think tank years earlier expressing his belief that the dramatic surge of mothers into the paid workforce had not been without costs to the American family. Socially conservative boilerplate, you might think, but the court found in the woman's favor and ordered BU to give her tenure, plus $215,000.

Congress never passed a law saying that university administrators are not allowed to dissent from feminist pieties. It was simply an unavoidable consequence of the legal revolution of the preceding fifty years. Freedoms that could be enforced by judges were expanded, which made the agents of this revolution feel that they were champions of liberty. They did not notice, or did not care, that the freedoms that had traditionally protected Americans *from* the scrutiny of judges were being trampled underfoot.

The legal revolution that allowed for this judicial intrusion into every aspect of life was similar to earlier revolutions in Supreme Court jurisprudence, but it was unlike them in one important way. The Industrial Revolution necessitated a greater level of economic regulation than had been envisioned by the Framers. Then railroads forced the federal government to take powers from the states as the economy became more national. There was no equivalent technological change that forced judges to start policing "hostile work environments" caused by the incivilities of rude bosses and coworkers, or the racial and gender balance of schools, universities, and workplaces. These kinds of laws would have been perfectly comprehensible to the Founding Fathers. They simply would have considered them a species of tyranny.

It has now reached the point where the internet meme "OK, Boomer," which in the fall of 2019 was big enough to warrant a trend piece in *The New York Times*, might fall under the shadow of antidiscrimination law. "If you have an employee, of any age, dropping the 'OK, Boomer' line against any employee who is over the age of 40, you have to take it seriously," warned one employment expert. It "can lead to patterns that create a hostile work environment, putting the company on the receiving end of a lawsuit." If it is true that expressing exasperation with baby boomers is really a form of unlawful discrimination, then I invite the EEOC to come to my office and serve me with an injunction.

8

THE MILLENNIALS

It's always the people who most hate the idea of turning into their parents who end up doing so. The millennials blame the boomers for wrecking the country, yet rather than break free from their influence, we continue seeing the world in their terms. Our social justice activists devote their lives to the same causes, with only the most minute updates in terminology but an agenda otherwise unchanged. Our rebels wear the same Che Guevara T-shirts, do the same drugs, obsess over the same music. I remember being surprised back in high school that the stoners cutting class behind the gym all had Black Sabbath and Pink Floyd patches on their jackets, and not anything more contemporary.

Worst of all, millennials seem intent on making the boomers' same mistakes. This is a book about the baby boom generation that has so far gone without mentioning the antiwar movement, Chicago 1968, Days of Rage, or long hot summers. For some people this is an unthinkable omission, because street protests were what the 1960s were all about. The reason for de-emphasizing street protests is, first of all, that they did not work. Adam Garfinkle's revisionist history of the antiwar movement, *Telltale Hearts*, notes that the protests had no effect on decision makers in the Johnson administration and little effect on public opinion, except to give second thoughts to the many Americans skeptical of the war but repulsed by Abbie Hoffman. Civil rights had fewer victories after the ghetto riots started, not more. One cannot even make a case for the street protests having had some deep cultural impact despite their political ineffectiveness, because for most participants it was nothing but a jolly interlude, after which they retired to the suburbs and a happy bourgeois life. The revolution did not come, and soon even Angela Davis grew up and got tenure.

Yet it is precisely this interlude that millennials are most determined to reenact. In the summer of 2020, when cities from Portland to Raleigh erupted in street violence and mobs looted storefronts, lobbed Molotov cocktails, and tore down public monuments, journalists rushed to compare it to 1968, with Joe Biden standing in for Hubert Humphrey and Antifa in the role of the yippies. The question on everyone's mind was whether the unrest would be as bad this time as it was fifty years ago. The answer is that it would be much worse, at least in its long-term effects, because all of the civilizational cushioning that gave boomers the leeway to act out without permanently destroying the country has been eroded. The only thing worse than a street protest that's all just fun and games is one that isn't.

The 1960s left Americans with an idea of street protest, even violent street protest, as something with minimal risks. You go to a march, have some fun, and raise some issues, and then the country goes back to normal. Of course, it is easy for us to say in hindsight that the 1960s were bound to turn out fine. At the time, there were serious people who worried that street revolts might lead to an actual revolution. The Kerner Commission, the federal inquiry into the causes of the urban riots of 1967, is famous for the line in its final report warning of two Americas, "one black, one white, separate and unequal." But before that, an earlier draft written by Lou Goldberg, a sociology grad student on the commission's Washington staff, was less sonorous but more chilling:

> The beginnings of guerrilla warfare of black youth against white power in the major cities of the United States: that is the direction that the present path is taking this country. . . . Twenty men, dedicated, committed, willing to risk death, and with intelligence and imagination could paralyze an entire city the size of New York or Chicago. . . . The history of Algeria or Cyprus could be the future history of America.

Bill Ayers was no Saadi Yacef, so Americans were spared the fate of the *pieds noirs*. There was no protracted war over urban territory, because middle-class families just moved to the suburbs. As for the boomer troublemakers themselves, they discovered when they aged out of their adolescent rebellion that there were good white-collar jobs waiting for them on the other side, underwritten by a strong economy favoring the college educated. The social stability that marked their 1950s childhoods had not yet been completely destroyed. Revolt never escalated into revolution because everyone had too much to gain from peace, the revolutionaries included.

Those stabilizing factors no longer obtain. The first and most obvious missing factor is prosperity. Boomers had nice suburban lives to retreat to. For millennials, one of the main engines of their rebellion is that their college degrees have not prevented them from falling down the economic ladder into low-level service jobs or the gig economy, all while still having to pay off college loans that go to fund an expanding army of middle-class administrators, many of whom, incidentally, are boomers. A French historian once quipped unkindly that Simone de Beauvoir "might have finished her life as a respectable housewife in Neuilly if wartime inflation had not destroyed the money intended to be her dowry." Whether or not that was true in her case, rebellion certainly becomes a more attractive option when people discover belatedly that they won't be living the lives they expected.

The boomers could venture to the political fringes because older generations with less taste for radicalism were still around to act as ballast on the ship of state. That silent majority no longer exists. A poll taken in 1968 found that only 10 percent of whites thought that police brutality was a major cause of riots in black neighborhoods. In the summer of 2020, support for the Black Lives Matter movement was high across all races, with more than two-thirds of Americans viewing the movement favorably, even after protests under its banner have led to vandalism, arson, and murder. How could it be controversial to support BLM when every member of the establishment is lining up to do the same, from Republican senators to Fortune 500 CEOs to the NFL commissioner? All the institutions that were a counterweight against disorder in the boomers' day have switched sides and joined the rioters' team.

It was sometimes noticed in the 1960s that Catholic youth were less likely than their peers to join the counterculture. Apart from the obvious reasons having to do with social class, I would guess one factor was that the fundamental attitude of the counterculture was, and is, very Protestant. You can only write off history as one long tale of oppression and every pre-boomer hero as a racist, sexist pig if you have no experience identifying with some continuously existing institution from the past, the way Catholics identify with the church. If you've never belonged to something, then you've never had to *defend* something, and that makes it easy to feel superior.

Today's young people don't belong to anything, never have, and never expect to. Growing up in the world the boomers made, millennials have gotten used to an America denuded of institutions. Old-fashioned virtues like loyalty not only aren't practiced; they are no longer considered virtues. You can be loyal to an institution—employer, school, your country of birth—to the extent that it conforms to your values and not one iota more, and those values are of course subject to change according to the latest fashions. After a century of revisionism and debunking, the only part of American history that millennials feel they are allowed to like or have pride in is the 1960s. So that's the part we're determined to imitate.

Which is fine with the boomers. They're still proud of what they did. When asked to describe his generation's accomplishments, Tom Hayden modestly replied, "We ended a war, toppled two presidents, and desegregated the South." Abbie Hoffman boasted in 1989, "We were young, we were reckless, arrogant, silly, headstrong—and we were right." The musician David Crosby's verdict is, by contrast, a model of self-criticism: "We were right about the war. We were right about the environment. We were right about civil rights and women's issues. But we were wrong about drugs."

The fools don't realize that they weren't right. They were just lucky. As this book has hopefully shown, the boomers leave behind a dismal legacy. In all the fields touched by the six boomers profiled here—technology, entertainment, economics, academia, politics, law—what they passed on to their children was worse than what they inherited. In some cases, as with Steve Jobs and his products or Camille Paglia and her books, they left behind accomplishments that are impressive and worthy of gratitude. But the overall effect of the boomer generation has still been essentially destructive.

Nostalgics like Hayden and Crosby remember it more rosily only because the cost of their destruction has mostly been borne by other people. Their rebellion took place at a time when America could afford to indulge a few rebels who wanted to run around and mouth off about burning the system down. There were enough sane people , with enough commitment to capitalism and democracy and the survival of the country they grew up in, that the system was never in any real danger. Now the boomers are encouraging their children to follow their example, but after more than half a century of boomers eroding the pillars of American stability, rebellion is not nearly as safe as it used to be.

The great 1969 BBC miniseries *Civilisation* ends on a note of naïveté. The host, Kenneth Clark, is wandering around the then newly built University of East Anglia, surrounded by boomer students hunched over their books or buzzing in conversation. "When I look at the world about me in the light of these programs, I don't at all feel as though we are entering on a new period of barbarism," he says. "In fact, I should doubt if so many people have ever been as well-fed, as well-read, as bright-minded and curious, and as critical as the young are today." He expresses his belief that although the young people of 1969 may "think poorly of existing institutions and want to abolish them," they will soon realize "it was institutions which made society work" and buckle down to carrying on the great Western tradition.

Such optimism, alas, was misplaced. Kenneth Clark was wrong about the boomers. They did not take their place in the chain of civilization. And if the boomers think that they can unmoor millennials from our past, immiserate our futures, tell us we're rich because we can afford iPhones but not families, teach us that narcissism is the highest form of patriotism, and still have a nation resilient enough to bounce back to normal after the younger generation starts to riot in the streets, then the boomers will be wrong about us.

Acknowledgments

The first person to read many of the chapters of this book was Daniel McCarthy, as director of the Robert Novak Journalism Fellowship at the Fund for American Studies. Without his suggestions, the book would be much worse than it is, and without TFAS's sponsorship, it would not have been written at all.

Other early readers include Andrew Ferguson, David Randall, Curtis Yarvin, and Christopher Caldwell. Their suggestions were priceless; all remaining errors are mine.

Before I wrote a book, I wrote magazine articles, and in that field I benefited from two great editors, the Matthews, Schmitz and Walther. As I considered graduating to book form, valuable encouragement and help came from Rusty Reno and Ross Douthat.

Thanks also go to Paul Beston, Jordan Bloom, Nick Burns, Johnny Burtka, Michael Brendan Dougherty, Hugo Gurdon, Elliot Kaufman, John Kienker, Seth Mandel, Barbara McClay, James Poulos, Roger Ream, Eve Tushnet, Tristyn and Kevin Wade, Ryan Williams, my agent William Callahan, and, of course, Bria Sandford and the team at Sentinel, for mentorship, professional assistance, and friendship.

It was a race to see which I would finish first, a book or a child, and Tim and I are glad that the winner, by the calendar and in our hearts, proved to be little Vlad. I only regret that my father did not live to see the debut of either one. This book is dedicated to him.

Notes

PREFACE

x "Only two things I find amuse me": Todd Avery, ed., *Unpublished Works of Lytton Strachey: Early Papers* (New York: Routledge, 2011), 65.

xi the nice thing about the 1920s: Martin B. Green, *Children of the Sun: A Narrative of "Decadence" in England After 1918* (Mount Jackson, Va.: Axios Press, 1976), 159.

CHAPTER 1: THE BOOMERS

2 a poll of millennials: Steve LeVine, "Millennials Blame Boomers for Ruining Their Lives," *Axios*, April 25, 2018, https://www.axios.com/51-of-millennials -blame-boomers-1524592674-0d20667a-c9e5-4e30-a430-3957e325a0d0.html.

4 one in five white women are on antidepressants: Laura H. Pratt et al., "Antidepressant Use Among Persons Aged 12 and Over: United States, 2011–2014," NCHS Data Brief 283 (Hyattsville, Md.: National Center for Health Statistics, 2017), 2.

4 Women have always worked: Amara Omeokwe, "Women Overtake Men as Majority of U.S. Workforce," *Wall Street Journal*, Jan. 10, 2020, https://www.wsj .com/articles/women-overtake-men-as-majority-of-u-s-workforce-11578670615.

4 Betty Friedan was a self-obsessed malcontent: Daniel Horowitz, *Betty Friedan and the Making of "The Feminine Mystique"* (Amherst: University of Massachusetts Press, 1998), 93.

5 **This gave young Gloria:** Gloria Steinem, *My Life on the Road* (New York: Random House, 2015), xxii.

5 **most respondents were satisfied:** Horowitz, *"The Feminine Mystique,"* 209.

5 **Polls of suburban housewives:** Helena Lopata, *Occupation: Housewife* (New York: Oxford University Press, 1971), 150–65.

6 **One in five white women:** Sara G. Miller, "1 in 6 Americans Takes a Psychiatric Drug," *Scientific American*, Dec. 13, 2016, https://www.scientific american.com/article/1-in-6-americans-takes-a-psychiatric-drug/.

6 **Most depressive episodes end:** Robert Whitaker, *Anatomy of an Epidemic: The Astonishing Rise of Mental Illness in America* (New York: Broadway Books, 2015), 168.

6 **"the champagne of drugs":** Ann Crittenden and Michael Ruby, "Cocaine: The Champagne of Drugs," *The New York Times Magazine*, Sept. 1, 1974.

6 **New Left historian Todd Gitlin:** Todd Gitlin, *The Sixties: Years of Hope, Days of Rage* (New York: Bantam Books, 1993), 215.

7 **Speaker of the House John Boehner:** Elizabeth Williamson, "John Boehner: From Speaker of the House to Cannabis Pitchman," *The New York Times*, June 3, 2019, https://www.nytimes.com/2019/06/03/us/politics/john-boehner -marijuana-cannabis.html.

7 **"We are a democracy":** Richard Hoggart, *The Uses of Literacy* (New York: Routledge, 2017), 168.

8 **"a bit of rabbit occasionally":** Richard Hoggart, *A Local Habitation: Life and Times, Volume 1, 1918–1940* (London: Chatto & Windus, 1988), 48.

9 **90 percent of American households:** Bruce Cannon Gibney, *A Generation of Sociopaths: How the Boomers Betrayed America* (New York: Hachette, 2017), 19.

9 **The Sunday Times called the Beatles:** Christopher Booker, *The Neophiliacs* (Boston: Gambit, 1970), 232.

9 **keep pop culture out of their countries:** Mary Fulbrook, *The People's State: East German Society from Hitler to Honecker* (New Haven, Conn.: Yale University Press, 2005), 131.

10 **"How A. E. Housman Invented Englishness":** Charles McGrath, "How A. E. Housman Invented Englishness," *The New Yorker*, June 19, 2017, https://www .newyorker.com/magazine/2017/06/26/how-ae-housman-invented-englishness.

10 "This tradition of segregation is discriminatory": Bruce J. Schulman, *The Seventies: The Great Shift in American Culture, Society, and Politics* (New York: Free Press, 2001), 10.

11 "If Yale was going to keep": Anne Gardiner Perkins, *Yale Needs Women: How the First Group of Girls Rewrote the Rules of an Ivy League Giant* (Naperville, Ill.: Sourcebooks, 2019), 16.

12 40 percent of births: Robert VerBruggen, "How We Ended Up with 40 Percent of Children Born out of Wedlock," IFStudies.org, Dec. 18, 2017, https://ifstudies.org/blog/how-we-ended-up-with-40-percent-of-children-born-out-of-wedlock; Robert Putnam, *Our Kids: The American Dream in Crisis* (New York: Simon & Schuster, 2015), 66.

12 in 1960, it was 95 percent: Charles Murray, *Coming Apart: The State of White America, 1960–2010* (New York: Crown, 2012), 170–71.

13 He was talking about the Old Left: Richard Vinen, *1968: Radical Protest and Its Enemies* (New York: HarperCollins, 2018), 29–30, 82–83.

14 "incompetent white people": Judith Stein, *Pivotal Decade: How the United States Traded Factories for Finance in the Seventies* (New Haven, Conn.: Yale University Press, 2010), chap. 1.

14 Richard Branson prevailed: Richard Vinen, *A History in Fragments: Europe in the Twentieth Century* (New York: Da Capo, 2001), 456.

15 "corporations are replacing churches": Tara Isabella Burton, "Are Corporations Becoming the New Arbiters of Public Morality?" *Vox*, Aug. 18, 2017.

15 "enjoy her possessions": Peter Oborne, *The Triumph of the Political Class* (New York: Simon & Schuster, 2007), 67–68.

15 "fight for the poor": Jacob Riis, *How the Other Half Lives: Studies Among the Tenements of New York* (Garden City, NY: Dover Thrift, 2009), 125.

CHAPTER 2: STEVE JOBS

19 Gizmodo had already given Apple its phone back: Yukari Iwatani Kane, *Haunted Empire: Apple After Steve Jobs* (New York: HarperCollins, 2014), 46–54.

20 iPhone is the top seller: Todd Hixon, "What Kind of Person Prefers an iPhone?," *Forbes*, April 10, 2014, https://www.forbes.com/sites/toddhixon/2014/04/10/what-kind-of-person-prefers-an-iphone/#25875c7fd1b0.

21 The revolution hadn't been lost: Michael S. Malone, *The Big Score: The Billion-Dollar Story of Silicon Valley* (New York: Doubleday, 1985), 373–74.

21 When he married Laurene Powell: Walter Isaacson, *Steve Jobs* (New York: Simon & Schuster, 2011), 273–74.

21 PR maven Regis McKenna: Randall Stross, *Steve Jobs and the NeXT Big Thing* (New York: Scribner, 1993), 211.

22 He ended up in the hospital: Erica Ho, "Steve Jobs' Fruitarian Diet Lands Ashton Kutcher in the Hospital," *Time*, Jan. 29, 2013, https://newsfeed.time .com/2013/01/29/steve-jobs-fruitarian-diet-lands-ashton-kutcher-in-the -hospital/.

22 Stanford Research Institute team: John Markoff, *What the Dormouse Said: How the 60s Counterculture Shaped the Personal Computer Industry* (New York: Viking, 2005), 91–92.

22 "Declaration of the Independence of Cyberspace": Fred Turner, *From Counterculture to Cyberculture: Stewart Brand, the Whole Earth Network, and the Rise of Digital Utopianism* (Chicago: University of Chicago Press, 2006); Edward Snowden, *Permanent Record* (New York: Henry Holt, 2019), 107.

22 Brand was the cameraman: Turner, *Counterculture to Cyberculture*, 110.

22 notorious 1972 *Rolling Stone* article: Adam Fisher, *Valley of Genius: The Uncensored History of Silicon Valley* (New York: Hachette, 2018), 46–47; Leslie Berlin, *Troublemakers: Silicon Valley's Coming of Age* (New York: Simon & Schuster, 2017), 225–27.

23 In 1985, Brand launched: Howard Rheingold, *The Virtual Community: Homesteading on the Digital Frontier* (Cambridge, Mass.: MIT Press, 2000), xvi.

23 "stay hungry, stay foolish": Isaacson, *Steve Jobs*, 56, 456.

23 "What we had was the Macintosh": Joe Nocera, *Good Guys and Bad Guys: Behind the Scenes with the Saints and Scoundrels of American Business (and Everything in Between)* (New York: Portfolio, 2008), 60.

23 "one person, one computer": Frank Rose, *West of Eden: The End of Innocence at Apple Computer* (New York: Stuyvesant Street Press, 1990), 38.

24 steal fire from the mountain: Jeff Goodell, "The Steve Jobs Nobody Knew," *Rolling Stone*, Oct. 27, 2011, https://www.rollingstone.com/culture/culture -news/the-steve-jobs-nobody-knew-71168/.

24 "smelled like infinity": John Sculley, with John A. Byrne, *Odyssey: Pepsi to Apple, a Journey of Adventure, Ideas, and the Future* (New York: Harper & Row, 1987), 150.

24 A French magazine: Michael Malone, *Infinite Loop: How the World's Most Insanely Great Computer Company Went Insane* (New York: Currency/Doubleday, 1999), 364.

24 "a total poseur": Owen W. Linzmayer, *Apple Confidential 2.0: The Definitive History of the World's Most Colorful Company* (San Francisco: No Starch Press, 2004), 134, 160.

25 he took the Apple advertising account: Linzmayer, *Apple Confiential 2.0*, 291.

25 His signature product: Brian McCullough, *How the Internet Happened: From Netscape to the iPhone* (New York: Liveright, 2018), 295.

25 He impressed Steve Jobs: Sculley, *Odyssey*, 29, 69–70.

25 stodgy and old-fashioned: Frederick Allen, *Secret Formula: The Inside Story of How Coca-Cola Became the Best-Known Brand in the World* (New York: Open Road Integrated Media, 2015), 294.

26 Steve Jobs was fired from Apple: Leslie Berlin, *Troublemakers: Silicon Valley's Coming of Age* (New York: Simon & Schuster, 2017), xi.

26 "a waste of time": Adam Lashinsky, *Inside Apple: How America's Most Admired—and Secretive—Company Really Works* (New York: Business Plus, 2012), 83.

26 Bill Gates's turn to philanthropy: Isaacson, *Steve Jobs*, 173.

26 "I've never voted": Margaret O'Mara, *The Code: Silicon Valley and the Remaking of America* (New York: Penguin, 2019), 195.

27 Sculley had been on the short list: Malone, *Infinite Loop*, 450.

27 "It's not about freedom": Isaacson, *Steve Jobs*, 516–17.

27 "to do what Hewlett": Isaacson, xix.

28 "Didn't your mother love you?": Chrisann Brennan, *The Bite in the Apple: A Memoir of My Life with Steve Jobs* (New York: St. Martin's Press, 2013), 16.

28 "He makes so much noise": Malone, *Infinite Loop*, 5.

28 too rebellious to work at Hewlett-Packard: Linzmayer, *Apple Confidential 2.0*, 76.

28 More than half of tech workers: Chantal da Silva, "H-1B Visa Row: Foreign Workers Make Up More than Half of Silicon Valley's Tech Industry, Reports Say," *Newsweek*, Jan. 18, 2018, https://www.newsweek.com/h-1b-visa-row-foreign-workers-make-more-half-silicon-valleys-tech-industry-784272.

28 visas for high-skilled workers: Michelle Malkin and John Miano, *Sold Out: How High-Tech Billionaires and Bipartisan Beltway Crapweasels Are Screwing America's Best and Brightest Workers* (New York: Threshold/Mercury Ink, 2015), 240–42.

29 Cheap labor from Asia: Ben Tarnoff, "Tech's Push to Teach Coding Isn't About Kids' Success, It's About Cutting Wages," *The Guardian*, Sept. 21, 2017, https://www.theguardian.com/technology/2017/sep/21/coding-education-teaching-silicon-valley-wages.

29 Kozmo's deliverymen were salaried: Tanner Hackett, "Why On-Demand Delivery Services Failed in the 90s," *Business Insider*, Sept. 14, 2014, http://www.businessinsider.com/on-demand-delivery-failed-in-the-90s-2014-9?op=1; Kara Platoni, "The Last Mile," *East Bay Express*, May 25, 2001, http://www.eastbayexpress.com/oakland/the-last-mile/Content?oid=1065476.

29 Dan Lyons joined a tech start-up: Dan Lyons, *Lab Rats: How Silicon Valley Made Work Miserable for the Rest of Us* (New York: Hachette, 2018).

30 "Ninety Hours a Week and Loving It": Isaacson, *Steve Jobs*, 124.

30 Apple had no pension plan: Malone, *Infinite Loop*, 294.

30 Google needed to cut benefits: Randall Stross, *Planet Google: One Company's Audacious Plan to Organize Everything We Know* (New York: Free Press, 2008), 17.

30 more dogs than children: Meredith May, "SF's Best Friend," *SFGate*, June 17, 2007, http://www.sfgate.com/news/article/S-F-S-BEST-FRIEND-Where-pooches-outnumber-2555688.php.

30 "wealth work": Marc Muro and Jacob Whiton, "Who's Employed by the Lifestyles of the Rich and Famous?," *The Avenue*, July 30, 2019, http://www.brookings.edu/blog/the-avenue/2019/07/15/whos-employed-by-the-lifestyles-of-the-rich-and-famous/.

31 Casino owners discovered: David T. Courtwright, *The Age of Addiction: How Bad Habits Became Big Business* (Cambridge, Mass.: Belknap Press, 2019), 195.

31 a third of homes had Nintendo: David Sheff, *Game Over: How Nintendo Conquered the World* (New York: Random House, 1993), 392.

31 "limbic capitalism": Courtwright, *Age of Addiction*, 6.

31 "universal basic income for the soul": Peter Suderman, "Young Men Are Playing Video Games Instead of Getting Jobs. That's Okay. (For Now.)," *Reason*, July 2017, https://reason.com/2017/06/13/young-men-are-playing-video-ga/.

32 He insisted that the Macintosh be built in America: Michael Anton, "The Frivolous Valley and Its Dreadful Conformity," *Law & Liberty*, Sept. 4, 2018, http://lawliberty.org/forum/the-frivolous-valley-and-its-dreadful-conformity.

32 NeXT pressured Jobs to outsource: Stross, *NeXT Big Thing*, 292.

32 Foxconn was first brought on: Leander Kahney, *Tim Cook: The Genius Who Took Apple to the Next Level* (New York: Portfolio, 2019), 73–77.

32 "China weighs more": Kane, *Haunted Empire*, 128.

33 "We actually did an evil scale": David A. Vise and Mark Malseed, *The Google Story: Inside the Hottest Business, Media, and Technology Success of Our Time*, 2nd ed. (New York: Bantam Books, 2018), 295.

33 Google tested forty-one variations: Ken Kocienda, *Creative Selection: Inside Apple's Design Process During the Golden Age of Steve Jobs* (New York: St. Martin's Press, 2018), 213.

33 "Did Alexander Graham Bell": Isaacson, *Steve Jobs*, 170.

33 everyone had a credit card: Joe Nocera, *A Piece of the Action: How the Middle Class Joined the Money Class* (New York: Simon & Schuster, 1994); Christopher Witko, "How Wall Street Became a Big Chunk of the U.S. Economy—and when the Democrats Signed On," *The Washington Post*, March 29, 2016, http://www.washingtonpost.com/news/monkey-cage/wp/2016/03/29/how-wall-street-became-a-big-chunk-of-the-u-s-economy-and-when-the-democrats-signed-on/.

34 the lifetime of the boomers: Louis Hyman, *Borrow: The American Way of Debt* (New York: Vintage, 2012).

34 "pedal pushers, or even dungarees": Hyman, 129–30.

35 "inclusion and diversity" report: Kahney, *Tim Cook*, 196.

35 an amicus brief: Chance Miller, "Apple Files Amicus Brief Supporting DACA and Dreamers, Signed by Tim Cook and Deirdre O'Brien," 9to5mac.com, Oct. 2, 2019.

35 Cook has been honored: Ben Lovejoy, "Apple Wins United Nations Award for Use of 100% Renewable Energy and More," 9to5mac.com, Sept. 26, 2019, https://9to5mac.com/2019/09/26/united-nations-award/; Chance Miller, "Tim Cook to Receive ADL 'Courage Against Hate' Award," 9to5mac.com, Nov. 14, 2018, https://9to5mac.com/2018/11/14/tim-cook-courage-against-hate-award/.

35 "I'm proud to be gay": Kahney, *Tim Cook*, 185.

36 he nearly lost his job: Paul Harris, "Niall Ferguson Apologises for Remarks About 'Gay and Childless' Keynes," *The Guardian*, May 4, 2013, http://www.theguardian.com/books/2013/may/04/niall-ferguson-apologises-gay-keynes.

37 deliberately (and painfully) cultivated impartiality: Taisuke Mitamura, *Chinese Eunuchs* (Rutland, Vt.: Tuttle Books, 1970); Norman A. Kutcher, *Eunuch and Emperor in the Great Age of Qing Rule* (Oakland: University of California Press, 2018).

37 "Why haven't we seen a photograph": Neil Maher, *Apollo in the Age of Aquarius* (Cambridge, Mass.: Harvard University Press, 2017), chap. 3.

37 Tim Cook's office contains photos: Kahney, *Tim Cook*, 25, 100.

38 "Having children really changes": Gary Wolf, "Steve Jobs: The Next Insanely Great Thing," *Wired*, Feb. 1996, http://www.wired.com/1996/02/jobs-2/.

38 "see themselves as global citizens": Chrystia Freeland, *Plutocrats: The Rise of the New Global Rich and the Fall of Everyone Else* (New York: Penguin Books, 2012), 78.

38 "transformation of the world economy": Chrystia Freeland, "The Rise of the New Global Elite," *The Atlantic*, Feb. 15, 2011, http://www.theatlantic.com/magazine/archive/2011/01/the-rise-of-the-new-global-elite/308343/.

39 "That's fucking history": Matt Sheehan, *The Transpacific Experiment: How China and California Collaborate and Compete for Our Future* (Berkeley, Calif.: Counterpoint, 2019), 180–81.

39 made the Chinese people less free: James Griffiths, *The Great Firewall of China: How to Build and Control an Alternative Version of the Internet* (London: Zed Books, 2018).

39 diminish admiration for China: François Bougon, *Inside the Mind of Xi Jinping* (London: C. Hurst, 2018); Charlotte Middlehurst, "Chinese President Snubs Mark Zuckerberg's Request for Baby Name," *The Telegraph* (London), Oct. 4, 2015, http://www.telegraph.co.uk/news/worldnews/asia/china/11910668/Chinese-president-snubs-Mark-Zuckerbergs-request-for-baby-name.html.

39 Shamelessly propagandistic ads for Huawei: Advertisement, *The Atlantic*, Nov. 2019, 50.

41 afraid of medical technology: Richard S. Tedlow, *The Watson Dynasty: The Fiery Reign and Troubled Legacy of IBM's Founding Father and Son* (New York: HarperCollins, 2003), 155–57.

41 "willed his death by refusing": Tedlow, 197.

41 Jobs wanted to try: Isaacson, *Steve Jobs*, 453.

41 " 'Revolutionize' ": Lashinsky, *Inside Apple*, 125.

CHAPTER 3: AARON SORKIN

43 this episode of *The West Wing*: Chris Lu, interview with Josh Malina and Hrishikesh Hirway, *West Wing Weekly*, Dec. 19, 2017, http://thewestwing weekly.com/episodes/410.

44 the majority of staffers on the Hill: Ashley Parker, "All the Obama 20-Somethings," *The New York Times Magazine*, April 29, 2010, https://www.nytimes.com/2010/05/02/magazine/02obamastaff-t.html; LegiStorm, "The 113th Congress by the Numbers (2013–2015)," https://www.legistorm .com/congress_by_numbers/index/by/senate/mode/age/term_id/4.html.

44 "If I have a talent": Aaron Sorkin, interview with Joshua Malina and Hrishikesh Hirway, *West Wing Weekly*, Sept. 20, 2016, http://thewestwingweekly .com/episodes/200; Aaron Sorkin, interview with Dan Rather, *The Big Interview with Dan Rather*, Sept. 16, 2013.

45 His father was a copyright lawyer: Aaron Sorkin, "A Tribute to Bernie Sorkin," *Journal of the Copyright Society of the USA* 64, no. 3 (Summer 2017): 295–307, https://cdn.ymaws.com/www.csusa.org/resource/resmgr/EU_/cpy_64 -3sorkin.pdf; Michael Schneider and Josef Adalian, "Sorkin to Nest at WBTV," *Variety*, July 26, 2000, https://variety.com/2000/tv/news/sorkin-to -nest-at-wbtv-1117784231/.

46 It's gonna change everything: Aaron Sorkin, *The Farnsworth Invention* (New York: Samuel French, 2009) p. 45, lines 5–7.

47 They wanted to turn him down: Aaron Sorkin, *West Wing* reunion panel at ATX Festival in Austin, Texas, June 15, 2016, http://thewestwingweekly.com/ episodes/001.

47 fire Chris Farley and Adam Sandler: James Andrew Miller and Tom Shales, *Live from New York: The Complete Uncensored History of "Saturday Night*

Live" as Told by Its Stars, Writers, and Guests (New York: Little, Brown, 2014), 415, 429.

48 "So what makes Aaron think": Tad Friend, "Laugh Riot," *The New Yorker*, Sept. 21, 1998, http://www.newyorker.com/magazine/1998/09/28/laugh-riot.

48 he gave Sorkin the green light: Lacey Rose, Michael O'Connell, and Marc Bernardin, "West Wing Uncensored," *The Hollywood Reporter*, May 13, 2014, http://www.hollywoodreporter.com/features/west-wing-uncensored-aaron-sorkin-703010.

48 "receptionist of the United States": Brian Abrams, *Obama: An Oral History 2009–2017* (New York: Little A, 2018), 65.

49 American Association of Political Consultants: Dennis W. Johnson, *Democracy for Hire: A History of American Political Consulting* (New York: Oxford University Press, 2017), 84, 315.

49 "You can't fall in love": Marc Levinson, *An Extraordinary Time: The End of the Postwar Boom and the Return of the Ordinary Economy* (New York: Basic Books, 2016), 21.

50 "busy-ness is a value in itself": Hedrick Smith, *The Power Game: How Washington Works* (New York: Ballantine, 1988), 108.

51 a mentally unstable murderer: Russell L. Riley, *Inside the Clinton White House: An Oral History* (New York: Oxford University Press, 2016), 201.

51 phrase from the *Communist Manifesto*: Gil Troy, *The Age of Clinton: America in the 1990s* (New York: Thomas Dunne Books, 2015), 25.

51 "the guy who eats all the ice cream": Riley, *Clinton White House*, 5, 14.

53 he thinks pop culture: Aaron Sorkin, interview with David Poland, *DP/30: The Oral History of Hollywood*, Nov. 2015, https://www.youtube.com/watch?v=fW-tCmR1_3A.

54 He hired Peggy Noonan: Rose, O'Connell, and Bernardin, "West Wing Uncensored."

55 This excellent system was responsible: Eli Attie, interview with Joshua Malina and Hrishikesh Hirway, *West Wing Weekly*, April 25, 2018.

55 "swinger when it comes to voting": Kristin Chenoweth, *A Little Bit Wicked: Life, Love, and Faith in Stages,* with Joni Rodger (New York: Touchstone, 2009), 20.

57 The show involved shackling a woman: Bill Carter, *Desperate Networks* (New York: Broadway Books, 2006), 60.

57 **"I'm not giving up"**: Salvador Hernandez, " 'SNL' Ditched the Laughs and Got Super Emotional," *BuzzFeed*, Nov. 12, 2016, https://www.buzzfeednews .com/article/salvadorhernandez/hallelujah.

58 **Victoria Jackson, the baby-voiced blonde**: Victoria Jackson, *Is My Bow Too Big? How I Went from "Saturday Night Live" to the Tea Party* (Powder Springs, Ga.: White Hall Press, 2012), chap. 3.

58 **Kristin Chenoweth got in trouble**: Chenoweth, *Little Bit Wicked*, 208.

59 **The only *SNL* cast member**: Jackson, *My Bow Too Big?*, chap. 4; Miller and Shales, *Live from New York*, 333–34.

59 **National Gas Association asked**: Thomas Doherty, *Cold War, Cool Medium: Television, McCarthyism, and American Culture* (New York: Columbia University Press, 2003), 66.

60 **"the values in New York City"**: Ashley Killough, "Donald Trump: Ted Cruz 'Has Hatred for New York,' " CNN.com, April 9, 2016, https://www .cnn.com/2016/04/09/politics/trump-cruz-new-york/index.html; Jeet Heer, "Ted Cruz Confirms that 'New York Values' Is Code for 'Jewish,' " *The New Republic*, Feb. 6, 2016, https://newrepublic.com/minutes/129338/ted-cruz -confirms-new-york-values-code-jewish.

63 **"You can change the players"**: Peter J. Boyer, *Who Killed CBS?* (New York: St. Martin's Press, 1989), 88, 370–71, 376.

65 **"courage" was one of his favorite words**: Boyer, 368–69; Ken Auletta, *Three Blind Mice: How the TV Networks Lost Their Way* (New York: Random House, 1991), 170.

66 **it was a way of rendering**: Amy Chozick, *Chasing Hillary: Ten Years, Two Presidential Campaigns, and One Intact Glass Ceiling* (New York: HarperCollins, 2018), 92.

67 **"Television is a gift of God"**: Boyer, *Who Killed CBS?*, 184.

68 **he's sticking to movies**: Ryan Gajewski, "Aaron Sorkin: I'm Done with TV After 'The Newsroom,' " *The Hollywood Reporter*, Nov. 8, 2014, https:// www.hollywoodreporter.com/news/aaron-sorkin-im-done-tv-747659.

CHAPTER 4: JEFFREY SACHS

69 **This diplomatic lie**: John Pollock, *Gordon: The Man Behind the Legend* (London: Constable, 1993).

70 "the infamous 'white man's burden'": Jeffrey Sachs, *The End of Poverty: Economic Possibilities for Our Time* (New York: Penguin, 2005), 43.

70 It was an order: Pollock, *Gordon*, 63.

71 "The Mussulman worships God": Pollock, 151.

71 "better to be tired and wait": Pollock, 153.

71 "If I thought the town wished": Pollock, 306.

71 Theodore Sachs: Nina Munk, *The Idealist: Jeffrey Sachs and the Quest to End Poverty* (New York: Doubleday, 2013), 9; John H. Richardson, "Jeffrey Sachs," *Esquire*, Dec. 1, 2003, https://classic.esquire.com/article/2003/12/1/jeffrey-sachs.

71 Sachs graduated summa cum laude: Munk, 11.

72 Harvard granted tenure to Larry Summers: Steven Pearlstein, "Tiff in the Economists' Temple," *The Washington Post*, April 5, 1998, https://www.washingtonpost.com/archive/business/1998/04/05/tiff-in-the-economists-temple/2b13ed4a-625a-4c3f-9666-0c968cb398af/.

72 some fresh scoop from Bolivia: Sachs, *End of Poverty*, 90–108.

73 U.S. ambassador Ben Stephansky: Frances R. Payne, *They Make Us Dangerous: Bolivia, 1964–1980* (Xlibris, 2012), chap. 5; Thomas C. Field, *From Development to Dictatorship: Bolivia and the Alliance for Progress in the Kennedy Era* (Ithaca, N.Y.: Cornell University Press, 2014), 198.

73 It was American Green Berets: Odd Arne Westad, *The Global Cold War: Third World Interventions and the Making of Our Times* (New York: Cambridge University Press, 2007), 178.

73 the Nazi "Butcher of Lyon": Benjamin Kohl and Linda Farthing, *Impasse in Bolivia: Neoliberal Hegemony and Popular Resistance* (New York: Zed Books, 2013), 51.

73 "Some of these philosophical debates": Jeffrey Sachs, interview with PBS's *Commanding Heights*, June 15, 2000, https://www.pbs.org/wgbh/commandingheights/shared/minitext/int_jeffreysachs.html.

74 That took three weeks: Gonzalo Sánchez de Lozada, interview with PBS's *Commanding Heights*, March 20, 2001, https://www.pbs.org/wgbh/commandingheights/shared/minitext/int_gonzalodelozada.html.

74 "Nobody leaves. No one talks to the press": Sachs, *End of Poverty*, 95.

74 most coups d'état in history: Kohl and Farthing, *Impasse in Bolivia*, 76, 37.

75 country still had no paved roads: Kohl and Farthing, 65.

75 "the Indiana Jones of economics": Leslie Wayne, "A Doctor for Struggling Economies," *The New York Times*, Oct. 1, 1989, https://www.nytimes.com/1989/10/01/business/a-doctor-for-struggling-economies.html.

75 their accounting system was incompatible: Elizabeth C. Dunn, *Privatizing Poland: Baby Food, Big Business, and the Remaking of Labor* (Ithaca, N.Y.: Cornell University Press, 2004), 41.

76 "Our Faults Are Known": Janine R. Wedel, "Introduction: *The Private Poland*, a Quarter Century Later," in *Prywatna Polska* (Warsaw: Trio, 2007), http://www.janinewedel.info/prywatna_polska_intro.html.

76 Poland's reward was to see: Jan Cienski, *Start-Up Poland: The People Who Transformed an Economy* (Chicago: University of Chicago Press, 2018).

77 investigators were able to confirm: Dunn, *Privatizing Poland*, 31.

77 "Professor Sachs visits Poland often": Janine R. Wedel, *Collision and Collusion: The Strange Case of Western Aid to Eastern Europe* (New York: St. Martin's Press, 2000), 209.

77 "Sometimes I get the idea": Sachs, *End of Poverty*, 109; Janine R. Wedel, "The Economist Heard Round the World," *World Monitor*, Oct. 1990, http://www.janinewedel.info/economheardWM.html.

78 "We worked on the Polish program": Leszek Balcerowicz, interview with PBS's *Commanding Heights*, Nov. 12, 2000, https://www.pbs.org/wgbh/commandingheights/shared/minitext/int_leszekbalcerowicz.html.

78 Figure out how fast: Wedel, "Economist."

78 "a smooth, confident manner": Wedel, *Collision and Collusion*, 47–48.

78 paid for by George Soros: Wedel, "Economist."

79 "the U.S. government is paying them": Janine R. Wedel, "Polish Officials Sour on US AID Approach," *The Christian Science Monitor*, March 2, 1992, http://www.janinewedel.info/topic_poland_CSMonitor92.pdf.

79 Sardonic officials joked: Wedel, *Collision and Collusion*, 45.

79 "Do I consider Russia a failure": Munk, *Idealist*, 17–18; John Donnelly, "The New Crusade," *The Boston Globe*, June 3, 2001, https://www.newspapers.com/newspage/442240031/.

80 Russia's GDP had dropped *by half*: Munk, 17.

80 "What I Did in Russia": Jeffrey Sachs, "What I Did in Russia," JeffSachs .org, March 14, 2012, archived at http://www.acamedia.info/politics/ukraine/ jeffrey_sachs/What_I_did_in_Russia.pdf.

80 receiving $40 million from USAID: David McClintick, "How Harvard Lost Russia," *Institutional Investor*, Jan. 13, 2006, https://www.institutionalinvestor .com/article/b150npp3q49x7w/how-harvard-lost-russia.

81 A fresh contract: Janine R. Wedel, "Who Taught Crony Capitalism to Russia?," *The Wall Street Journal*, March 19, 2001, https://www.wsj.com/ articles/SB984947892753855394.

81 "a young man and woman": Angus Roxburgh, *Moscow Calling: Memoirs of a Foreign Correspondent* (Edinburgh: Birlinn, 2017), chap. 29.

81 engage in Ugly American behavior: Japhy Wilson, *Jeffrey Sachs: The Strange Case of Dr. Shock and Mr. Aid* (New York: Verso, 2014), 30.

82 He managed to keep his faculty position at Harvard: McClintick, "Harvard Lost Russia."

82 Summers and Shleifer were always: McClintick.

83 "Communism was falling": Richardson, "Jeffrey Sachs."

83 "He was clearly capable": Sylvia Nasar, "Three Whiz Kid Economists of the 90's, Pragmatists All," *The New York Times*, Oct. 27, 1991, https://www .nytimes.com/1991/10/27/business/three-whiz-kid-economists-of-the-90-s -pragmatists-all.html.

83 For two years he supervised: Sachs, *End of Poverty*, 203.

85 "you don't need millions of dollars to fix this": Munk, *Idealist*, 30.

85 He campaigned for donations: Wilson, *Jeffrey Sachs*, 81.

86 "I am the same person": Amy Wilentz, "Jeffrey Sachs's Grand Experiment," *Condé Nast Traveler*, August 12, 2008, https://www.cntraveler.com/stories/ 2008-08-12/jeffrey-sachs-s-grand-experiment.

86 "For the record, he's a bully": Munk, *Idealist*, 33.

86 He attempted to defend: Pearlstein, "Economists' Temple."

87 "He's a punk!": Munk, *Idealist*, 100, 102.

87 "Children are dying": Wilson, *Jeffrey Sachs*, 68.

87 "I advise Africa's governments": Munk, *Idealist*, 140.

87 "Your actions are reprehensible!": Munk, 102–3.

NOTES

87 **"I was really shaken up"**: Paul Starobin, "Does It Take a Village?," *Foreign Policy*, June 24, 2013, https://foreignpolicy.com/2013/06/24/does-it-take-a-village/.

88 **the Millennium Villages project keeps**: Wilson, *Jeffrey Sachs*, 89.

88 **One peer-reviewed *Lancet* paper**: Paul Pronyk, "Errors in a Paper on the Millennium Villages Project," *Lancet* 379, no. 9830 (May/June 2012): 1946, https://doi.org/10.1016/S0140-6736(12)60824-1; Wilson, *Jeffrey Sachs*, 130.

88 **But such direct hits are rare**: Joe Nocera, "Fighting Poverty, and Critics," *The New York Times*, Sept. 3, 2013, https://www.nytimes.com/2013/09/03/opinion/nocera-fighting-poverty-and-critics.html; Jeffrey Sachs, "Letter: Millennium Villages Project," *The New York Times*, Sept. 6, 2013.

88 **Planners don't know**: William Easterly, *The White Man's Burden: Why the West's Efforts to Aid the Rest Have Done So Much Ill and So Little Good* (New York: Penguin, 2006).

89 **Easterly has condemned**: Easterly, 24.

90 **"America won't help England"**: Elliott Roosevelt, *As He Saw It* (New York: Duell, Sloane, and Pearce, 1946), 25.

90 **"erect dikes to contain it"**: Michael E. Latham, *The Right Kind of Revolution: Modernization, Development, and U.S. Foreign Policy from the Cold War to the Present* (Ithaca, N.Y.: Cornell University Press, 2011), 41

90 **Persian verse**: Michael O'Dwyer, *India as I Knew It, 1885–1925* (London: Constable, 1925), 34.

91 **United States even gave Nasser**: Michael Doran, *Ike's Gamble: America's Rise to Dominance in the Middle East* (New York: Free Press, 2016), 83.

91 **America signaled its support**: Hilaire du Berrier, *Background to Betrayal: The Tragedy of Vietnam* (Boston: Western Islands, 1965), 101.

92 **Their new leaders were tyrants**: D. K. Fieldhouse, *Black Africa, 1945–1980: Economic Decolonization and Arrested Development* (New York: Routledge, 2011), 32.

92 **Ghana's cocoa production had declined**: Fieldhouse, 145.

92 **"empire" is an ancient term**: Krishan Kumar, *Visions of Empire: How Five Imperial Regimes Shaped the World* (Princeton, N.J.: Princeton University Press, 2017), 16.

93 "Alianza para Progreso": Stephen G. Rabe, *The Most Dangerous Area in the World: John F. Kennedy Confronts Communist Revolution in Latin America* (Chapel Hill: University of North Carolina Press, 1999), 15.

93 most sought-after Africa hands: Taylor Mayol, "He Helped Unseat the Gambian Dictator—Who's Next?," *Ozy*, March 25, 2017, https://www.ozy .com/around-the-world/he-helped-unseat-the-gambian-dictator-whos-next/ 75821/; Krista Mahr, "How an American Consultancy Helped Oust Gambia's Dictator," *Newsweek*, Jan. 30, 2017, https://www.newsweek.com/2017/03/03/ gambia-yahya-jammeh-adama-barrow-vanguard-550031.html.

93 "these guys have only one idea": David Rieff, *A Bed for the Night: Humanitarianism in Crisis* (New York: Simon & Schuster, 2002), 118.

94 head of the Kosovo Liberation Army: Mark Moyar, *Aid for Elites: Building Partner Nations and Ending Poverty Through Human Capital* (New York: Cambridge University Press, 2016), 82.

94 Groups like Freedom House: Lincoln A. Mitchell, *The Democracy Promotion Paradox* (Washington, D.C.: Brookings Institution Press, 2016), 9.

95 "It will be a black day for the human race": George Santayana, *Soliloquies in England, and Later Soliloquies* (London: Constable, 1922), 32.

95 "When I started my career": Jeffrey Sachs, "The End of American Exceptionalism," remarks at the Oxford Union, video, 52:54, Oct. 6, 2017, https:// www.youtube.com/watch?v=ExT9tlerC6c.

95 Lord Derby reassured Benjamin Disraeli: John Campbell, *Pistols at Dawn: Two Hundred Years of Political Rivalry from Fox and Pitt to Blair and Brown* (London: Vintage, 2009), 104.

96 "There are times now that he appears to be closer to St. Francis than to Balcerowicz": Tadeusz Kowalik, *From Solidarity to Sellout: The Restoration of Capitalism in Poland* (New York: Monthly Review Press, 2011), 72.

CHAPTER 5: CAMILLE PAGLIA

98 Sontag was goaded into responding: Camille Paglia, *Vamps and Tramps: New Essays* (New York: Vintage, 1994), 344–60.

99 "the end of the Latin world": Koenraad Swart, *The Sense of Decadence in Nineteenth-Century France* (Dordrecht: Springer, 1964), 124.

100 "I follow the Decadents: Camille Paglia, *Sexual Personae: Art and Decadence from Nefertiti to Emily Dickinson* (New Haven, Conn.: Yale University Press, 1990), 428.

102 "His battles are my battles": Camille Paglia, *Sex, Art, and American Culture: Essays* (New York: Vintage, 1992), xi.

102 She arrived at Yale: Paglia, *Vamps and Tramps*, 119.

103 "Everyone else had been hired": Heather Findley, "Paglia 101," *Girlfriends*, Sept. 2000.

103 she proceeded in 1972: Paglia, *Vamps and Tramps*, 347.

103 Paglia was into witchcraft: Deanne Stillman, "The Many Masks of Camille Paglia," *Los Angeles Times Magazine*, Feb. 16, 1992, http://www.latimes.com/archives/la-xpm-1992-02-16-tm-4660-story.html.

103 "went ballistic, and attacked me": Findley, "Paglia 101."

104 "silence, exile, and cunning": Francesca Stanfill, "Woman Warrior: Sexual Philosopher Camille Paglia Jousts with the Politically Correct," *New York*, March 4, 1991, 27, http://www.francescastanfill.squarespace.com/warrior-woman-new-york-march.

104 Showalter would later pan *Sexual Personae*: Elaine Showalter, "The Divine Miss P," *London Review of Books*, Feb. 11, 1993, vol 15, no 3, http://www.lrb.co.uk/the-paper/v15/n03/elaine-showalter/the-divine-miss-p.

104 "the Leona Helmsley of Harvard": Stanfill, "Woman Warrior," 29.

104 "pedestrian critical skills": Paglia, *Sex, Art, and American Culture*, 220.

104 "Many of us, through folly, hubris, or mischance": Paglia, 246.

104 "America's current intellectual crisis": Paglia, *Vamps and Tramps*, 97.

105 That edition stayed on the *New York Times*: Stillman, "Masks of Camille Paglia"; Stanfill, "Woman Warrior," 24.

105 The latter was particularly provoking: Paglia, *Vamps and Tramps*, 3.

106 she got into a tabloid scrap: Paglia, 436.

106 *Spin* asked her about battered wives: Paglia, *Vamps and Tramps*, 124.

106 "everyone knows throughout the world": Paglia, *Sex, Art, and American Culture*, 63.

106 "I am a pornographer": Paglia, *Vamps and Tramps*, 107.

107 So was launched a long: Charles Rembar, *The End of Obscenity: The Trials of Lady Chatterley, Tropic of Cancer, and Fanny Hill by the Lawyer Who Defended Them* (New York: Random House, 1968), 14–17.

108 "the concept did not exist at all": Rembar, *End of Obscenity*, 4.

108 In the British *Chatterley* case: C. H. Rolph, *The Trial of Lady Chatterley: Regina v. Penguin Books Limited* (London: Penguin, 1961), 6.

109 *Fanny Hill* held a respectable place: *A Book Named "John Cleland's Memoirs of a Woman of Pleasure" v. Massachusetts*, 383 U.S. 413 (1966).

109 This defense proved successful: Rembar, *End of Obscenity*, 4, 436.

109 the Roman Catholic Church withdrew: Una Cadegan, *All Good Books Are Catholic Books: Print Culture, Censorship, and Modernity in Twentieth-Century America* (Ithaca, N.Y.: Cornell University Press, 2013), 195.

110 The commission's final report: David Friend, *The Naughty Nineties: The Triumph of the American Libido* (New York: Grand Central Publishing, 2017), 409.

110 in the back of *Penthouse*: Frederick S. Lane, *Obscene Profits: The Entrepreneurs of Pornography in the Cyber Age* (New York: Routledge, 2001), 280.

110 73 percent of Americans: *Technical Report of the Commission on Obscenity and Pornography, Volume VI: National Survey* (Washington, D.C.: Government Printing Office, 1971), 92, 95, 99.

111 "What attracted me to gay men": Paglia, *Vamps and Tramps*, 103.

111 "We've watched gay porn together": John Gallagher, "Attack of the 50-Foot Lesbian," *The Advocate*, Oct. 18, 1994, 44, http://connection.ebscohost.com/c/articles/9610487/attack-50-foot-lesbian.

111 She credits him with being: Paglia, *Vamps and Tramps*, 202–7.

111 pitch-black orgy rooms and sex shows: Paglia, 104.

111 writer Samuel R. Delany: Samuel R. Delany, *Red Times Square, Blue Times Square* (New York: New York University Press, 1999), 29.

112 Hedren rejected the widespread theories: Camille Paglia, *The Birds* (London: British Film Institute, 1998), 16–17.

113 'Pagan goddess!' I want to call out: Paglia, *Vamps and Tramps*, 58–59.

113 "sugar-coated Shirley Temple nonsense": Paglia, *Sex, Art, and American Culture*, 49.

114 *Free Women, Free Men*: Camille Paglia, *Free Women, Free Men: Sex, Gender, Feminism* (New York: Pantheon, 2017).

114 "fine netting for veils": Camille Paglia, *Break, Blow, Burn: Camille Paglia Reads Forty-three of the World's Best Poems* (New York: Pantheon, 2005), 99.

114 What Bloom fails to mention: Donald Alexander Downs, *Cornell '69: Liberalism and the Crisis of the American University* (Ithaca, N.Y.: Cornell University Press, 1999), 271–72.

115 "toadying careerists, Fifties types": Paglia, *Sex, Art, and American Culture*, viii.

117 "Scholarship is an ideal and a calling": Paglia, 233.

117 The first ever professor: Alvin B. Kernan, *Death of Literature* (New Haven, Conn.: Yale University Press, 1990), 1.

119 "of a class of twenty-five students": Emily Esfahani Smith, "My Camille Paglia Interview: The Outtakes," *Acculturated*, Dec. 17, 2012.

119 Paglia was the one chosen: Neil Postman and Camille Paglia, "She Wants Her TV! He Wants His Book!," *Harper's Magazine*, March 1991, https://harpers.org/archive/1991/03/she-wants-her-tv-he-wants-his-book/.

121 "movies, television, sports, and rock music": Paglia, *Sexual Personae*, xiii.

121 By the time *Vamps and Tramps* was released in 1994: Paglia, *Vamps and Tramps*, xiv.

123 If her latter successor would like: Mary McCarthy, "Time: The Weekly Fiction Magazine," *Fact* 1, no. 1 (Jan/Feb. 1964): 7.

CHAPTER 6: AL SHARPTON

125 In the book he wrote: Al Sharpton, *Al on America*, with Karen Hunter (New York: Kensington, 2002), xv.

125 Sharpton summarizes Burns's dichotomy: Al Sharpton, *The Rejected Stone: Al Sharpton and the Path to American Leadership*, with Nick Chiles (New York: Simon & Schuster, 2013), 128.

125 "While Dr. King was fighting": Sharpton, 128.

126 "They bash me at Fox News": Carl F. Horowitz, *Sharpton: A Demagogue's Rise* (Falls Church, Va.: National Legal and Policy Center, 2014), 7.

128 forced to relocate: Elizabeth Kolbert, "The People's Preacher," *The New Yorker*, Feb. 18, 2002 156, https://www.newyorker.com/magazine/2002/02/18/the-peoples-preacher; Michael Klein, *The Man Behind the Sound Bite: The Real Story of the Rev. Al Sharpton* (New York: Castillo International, 1991), 38.

129 "Reverend, how many times do I have to tell you": Al Sharpton, *Go and Tell Pharaoh: The Autobiography of the Reverend Al Sharpton* (New York: Doubleday, 1996), 68–69.

129 "business apartheid": Klein, *Sound Bite*, 82, 128–30.

130 the Sicilians were fed, clothed, and housed worse: Booker T. Washington, *The Man Farthest Down* (New York: Doubleday, 1912).

130 Tammany would have loved to add blacks: John Christopher Walter, *The Harlem Fox: J. Raymond Jones and Tammany, 1920–1970* (Albany: State University of New York Press, 1989), 2–3.

131 Harlem's population of 225,000: Harold Cruse, *The Crisis of the Negro Intellectual* (New York: New York Review Books, 2005), 81.

131 "someone had written a book": Sharpton, *Go and Tell Pharaoh*, 33.

131 His constituents didn't care: Charles V. Hamilton, *Adam Clayton Powell: The Political Biography of an American Dilemma* (New York: Atheneum, 1991).

132 he sponsored the political careers: Walter, *Harlem Fox*.

132 "That is a complete lie": Hamilton, *Adam Clayton Powell*, 272.

133 Powell allowed the boy: Klein, *Sound Bite*, 55–56.

134 "But for our primary target," King declared: Mary Lou Finley et al., ed., *The Chicago Freedom Movement: Martin Luther King Jr. and Civil Rights Activism in the North* (Lexington, Ky.: University Press of Kentucky, 2016), 45–46.

135 Chicago's black population had exploded: Martin L. Deppe, *Operation Breadbasket: An Untold Story of Civil Rights in Chicago 1966–1971* (Athens, Ga.: University of Georgia Press, 2017), 3.

135 Welfare workers were forbidden: Adam Cohen and Elizabeth Taylor, *American Pharaoh: Mayor Richard J. Daley, His Battle for Chicago and the Nation* (New York: Little, Brown, 2000).

135 **These were no Uncle Toms:** Deppe, *Operation Breadbasket*, 10; David Remnick, *The Bridge: The Life and Rise of Barack Obama* (New York: Knopf, 2010), 155.

136 **"My precinct captain":** Barbara Reynolds, *Jesse Jackson: America's David* (Washington, D.C.: JFJ Associates, 1985), 188–89.

136 **"The Negroes of Chicago":** Gary Rivlin, *Fire on the Prairie: Harold Washington, Chicago Politics, and the Roots of the Obama Presidency* (Philadelphia: Temple University Press, 2013).

136 **Hosea Williams disrupted Mass:** Sharpton, *Go and Tell Pharaoh*, 59.

136 **The mayor accommodated:** Cohen and Taylor, *American Pharaoh*.

137 **Daley sent out all his inspectors:** Marshall Frady, *Martin Luther King Jr · A Life* (New York: Penguin, 2005), 172.

138 **Even a peaceful boycott:** Paul D. Moreno, *From Direct Action to Affirmative Action: Fair Employment Law and Policy in America, 1933–1972* (Baton Rouge: Louisiana State University Press, 1997), 37–41; Ken I. Kersch, *Constructing Civil Liberties: Discontinuities in the Development of American Constitutional Law* (New York: Cambridge University Press, 2004), 145, 212.

139 **the firm National Tea:** Reynolds, *Jesse Jackson*, 119–22.

140 **"You have to understand, I'm special":** Marshall Frady, *Jesse: The Life and Pilgrimage of Jesse Jackson* (New York: Simon & Schuster, 1996), 185, 203.

140 **"disenfranchising over 900,000 voters":** Warren Weaver Jr., "Panel Denies Convention Seats to 59 Daley Delegates," *The New York Times*, July 1, 1972, https://www.nytimes.com/1972/07/01/archives/panel-denies-convention-seats -to-59-daley-delegates-their-places.html.

141 **he came back to town:** Remnick, *The Bridge*, 259–61; David Garrow, *Rising Star: The Making of Barack Obama* (New York: William Morrow, 2017).

141 **That agreement can involve:** Kenneth R. Timmerman, *Shakedown: Exposing the Real Jesse Jackson* (New York: Regnery, 2013).

142 **General Motors wrote its first check:** Isabel Vincent and Melissa Klein, "How Sharpton Gets Paid Not to Cry 'Racism' at Corporations," *New York Post*, January 4, 2015, https://nypost.com/2015/01/04/how-sharpton-gets -paid-to-not-cry-racism-at-corporations/.

142 **Sharpton was given his own show:** Wayne Barrett, "Al Sharpton: Affirmative-Action Beneficiary of the NBC-Comcast Merger?," *The Daily Beast*, July 13,

2017, https://www.thedailybeast.com/al-sharpton-affirmative-action-beneficiary -of-the-nbc-comcast-merger.

143 a predominantly black jury: Sharpton, *Go and Tell Pharaoh*, 149–52; "N.Y. Jury Clears Sharpton of Theft Charges," *The Washington Post*, July 2, 1990, https://www.washingtonpost.com/archive/politics/1990/07/03/ny-jury -clears-sharpton-of-theft-charges/20a669f1-ffda-405c-9da5-80b64c33061c/.

143 IRS and the state of New York: Chuck Bennett, "Rev. Al's Half-Price Deal on $1.8M Taxes," *New York Post*, March 28, 2009, https://nypost.com/ 2009/03/28/rev-als-half-price-deal-on-1-8m-taxes/.

144 "the policy is merely 'private' ": Bernard Schwartz, *The Unpublished Opinions of the Warren Court* (New York: Oxford University Press, 1985), 172.

144 "The choice of the proprietor": Jack Greenberg, *Crusaders in the Courts: How a Dedicated Band of Lawyers Fought for the Civil Rights Revolution* (New York: Basic Books, 1994), 312.

145 A teacher at McKinley High: *Investigation of Public School Conditions*, Hearing before the Subcommittee to Investigate Public School Standards and Conditions and Juvenile Delinquency in the District of Columbia, 84th Congress (1956).

146 superintendent Carl F. Hansen: Carl F. Hansen, *Danger in Washington: The Story of My Twenty Years in the Public Schools in the Nation's Capital* (Parker Publishing, 1968); Raymond Wolters, *Burden of Brown: Thirty Years of School Desegregation* (Knoxville, Tenn.: University of Tennessee Press, 1992.

148 he learned about Pannell's gun: Mike Kelly, *Color Lines: The Troubled Dreams of Racial Harmony in an American Town* (New York: William Morrow, 1995).

148 in *Go and Tell Pharaoh*: Sharpton, *Go and Tell Pharaoh*, 118.

149 dark psychological forces: Horowitz, *Sharpton*, 67–76; Jim Sleeper, *Closest of Strangers: Liberalism and the Politics of Race in New York* (New York: Norton, 1991).

149 "I do not bring down property values when I move in": James Baldwin and Randall Kenan, *The Cross of Redemption: Uncollected Writings* (New York: Pantheon, 2010), 61.

149 Ta-Nehisi Coates: Ta-Nehisi Coates, *Between the World and Me* (New York: Spiegel & Grau, 2015), 79.

150 "fear for their lives": Hillel Levine and Lawrence Harman, *The Death of an American Jewish Community: A Tragedy of Good Intentions* (Lexington, Mass.: Plunkett Lake Press, 2012).

150 New York's city government played a similar role: Sleeper, *Closest of Strangers.*

151 "I am locked up like in the ghettos of Europe": Jonathan Rieder, *Canarsie: The Jews and Italians of Brooklyn against Liberalism* (Harvard University Press, 1985).

151 The Ebsteins quickly moved: Jonathan Kaufman, *Broken Alliance: The Turbulent Times Between Blacks and Jews in America* (New York: Touchstone, 1995), 165–193.

152 "Maybe I'm jaded": Ta-Nehisi Coates, "The Beef at McCarran Pool," *The Atlantic*, July 5, 2012, https://www.theatlantic.com/national/archive/2012/07/the-beef-at-mccarren-pool/259448/.

153 Jackson was effectively banned: Remnick, *The Bridge*; Michael Eric Dyson, *The Black Presidency: Barack Obama and the Politics of Race in America* (New York: Mariner Books, 2017).

154 Sharpton was careful: Horowitz, *Sharpton.*

155 "I now have a problem": Keeanga-Yamahtta Taylor, *From #BlackLivesMatter to Black Liberation* (Chicago: Haymarket Books, 2016).

155 "a bona fide black leader": Horowitz, *Sharpton*, 26.

155 When Sharpton ran for mayor: Evan Mandery, *Eyes on City Hall: A Young Man's Education in New York City Political Warfare* (New York: Routledge, 2018).

156 "They don't know what the laws are": Arthur Schlesinger, *Robert Kennedy and His Times* (New York: Mariner, 2002), 334.

156 "To be a Negro in this country": Remnick, *The Bridge*, 172.

157 When he testified: Baldwin, *Cross of Redemption*, 109–119.

157 "I'm just so lonely": David Adams Leeming, *James Baldwin: A Biography* (New York: Arcade, 1994), 368.

158 "They sent him two tickets": Arthur M. Schlesinger Jr., *Journals 1952–2000* (New York: Penguin, 2007), 520.

160 **Conservatives have erred for decades:** Daniel Golden, "Barriers Students Faced Count in University Admission Process," *The Wall Street Journal*, July 12, 2002, https://www.wsj.com/articles/SB102642240213450520.

161 **nearly one in thirteen D.C. residents:** Harry Jaffe and Tom Sherwood, *Dream City: Race, Power, and the Decline of Washington, D.C.* (New York: Simon & Schuster, 1994), 210.

CHAPTER 7: SONIA SOTOMAYOR

165 **circulated a blistering draft dissent:** Joan Biskupic, *Breaking In: The Rise of Sonia Sotomayor and the Politics of Justice* (New York: Sarah Crichton Books, 2014), 205–10.

166 **"I would soon see a version of it":** "May It Displease the Court: Race and Justice Sotomayor," *ProPublica*, July 8, 2015, https://www.propublica.org/article/may-it-displease-the-court-race-and-justice-sotomayor.

166 **Justices don't always read:** Biskupic, *Breaking In*, 210.

167 **Race matters because of the slights:** *Schuette v. Coalition to Defend Affirmative Action et al.*, 572 U.S. 291 (2014).

167 **"the Greenhouse Effect":** Edward Lazarus, *Closed Chambers: The Rise, Fall, and Future of the Modern Supreme Court* (New York: Penguin Books, 2005), 428, 528.

167 **a reported $1.175 million advance:** Biskupic, *Breaking In*, 245.

167 **in front of middle schoolers:** Sonia Sotomayor, "Diversity and the Legal Profession," Aug. 26, 2010, University of Denver, transcript and C-SPAN video, 57:30, https://www.c-span.org/video/?295200-1/diversity-legal-profession.

167 **Sotomayor has shaped her persona:** Bernard Schwartz, *Super Chief: Earl Warren and His Supreme Court* (New York: New York University Press, 1983), 215–17.

169 **"The facts imply and reflect":** Sonia Sotomayor, letter to the editor, "Anti-Latino Discrimination at Princeton," *The Daily Princetonian*, May 10, 1974, 55, http://dailyprincetonian.com/news/2009/05/letter-to-the-editor-anti-latino-discrimination-at-princeton-may-10-1974/.

169 **HEW sent a federal official to New Jersey:** Mendy Fisch, "Sotomayor '76 Shapes U. Affirmative Action Practices," *The Daily Princetonian*, Sept. 14, 2009, https://affirmact.blogspot.com/2009/09/.

170 **Sotomayor sent her letter:** "A History of the Journey from the Third World Center to the Carl A. Fields Center for Cultural Understanding," http://fieldscenter.princeton.edu/history.

170 **"admitted to Yale Law School":** Sonia Sotomayor, *My Beloved World* (New York: Alfred A. Knopf, 2013), 188.

170 **"They really put it to him":** Joan Biskupic, *American Original: The Life and Constitution of Supreme Court Justice Antonin Scalia* (New York: Sarah Crichton Books, 2009), 30.

171 **she had handled the questioning:** Sotomayor, *My Beloved World*, 189–90.

171 **the German Legal Aid Society:** Earl Johnson Jr., *Justice and Reform: The Formative Years of the OEO Legal Services Program* (New York: Russell Sage Foundation, 1974), 4.

171 **The Mexican American Legal Defense and Educational Fund:** *Balancing the Scales of Justice: Financing Public Interest Law in America* (Washington, D.C.: Council for Public Interest Law, 1976).

172 **By 1975, there were six hundred:** Nan Aron, *Liberty and Justice for All: Public Interest Law in the 1980s and Beyond* (New York: Taylor & Francis, 1989), 33.

172 *Serrano v. Priest:* Robert Reinhold, "John Serrano, et al., and School Tax Equality," *The New York Times*, Jan. 10, 1972, https://www.nytimes.com/1972/01/10/archives/john-serrano-jr-et-al-and-school-tax-equality-serrano-jr-et-al-and.html; *Scales of Justice*, 189–90.

172 **The Puerto Rican Legal Defense:** *Scales of Justice*, 197–99.

173 **This, too, is to ensure:** *NAACP v. Button*, 371 U.S. 415 (1963) (Harlan dissenting).

173 **When the EEOC decided:** James D. Keeney, *Enforcing the Civil Rights Act: Fighting Racism, Sexism, and the Ku Klux Klan: The Story of the Miami EEOC's First Class Action Trial* (Sarasota, Fla.: Civil Rights Publishing, 2012).

173 **The Supreme Court ruled:** *In re Primus*, 436 U.S. 412 (1978).

173 **"earnest and vital controversy":** Alexander Bickel, *The Unpublished Opinions of Mr. Justice Brandeis* (Chicago: University of Chicago Press, 1967), 3.

174 **An EEOC case filed in 1973:** Frederick R. Lynch, *Invisible Victims: White Males and the Crisis of Affirmative Action* (New York: Praeger, 1991), 45–47.

174 More than 500,000 pro-choice protesters: Gil Troy, *The Age of Clinton: America in the 1990s* (New York: Thomas Dunne Books, 2015), 68.

174 When the *Casey* decision came down: *Planned Parenthood of Southeastern Pennsylvania v. Casey*, 505 U.S. 833 (1992).

175 "There were private questions": Biskupic, *Breaking In*, 165.

175 Anthony Kennedy remembers: Jan Crawford Greenburg, *Supreme Conflict: The Inside Story of the Struggle for Control of the United States Supreme Court* (New York: Penguin, 2007), 61.

175 staffers also told Jeffrey Toobin: Jeffrey Toobin, *The Oath: The Obama White House and the Supreme Court* (New York: Doubleday, 2012), 226.

175 "she's not nearly as smart": Ed Whelan, "Tribe to Obama: Sotomayor Is 'Not Nearly as Smart as She Seems to Think She Is,'" National Review Online, Oct. 28, 2010, https://www.nationalreview.com/bench-memos/tribe -obama-sotomayor-not-nearly-smart-she-seems-think-she-ed-whelan/.

176 "She's a fine Second Circuit judge": Jeffrey Rosen, "The Case Against Sotomayor," *The New Republic*, May 4, 2009.

176 Tribe and Rosen had both defended: Jeffrey Rosen, *The Most Democratic Branch: How the Courts Serve America* (New York: Oxford University Press, 2006), 78–80.

176 It probably did not occur to Professor Tribe: Peter Melnick, "Professors, Administrators Debate Affirmative Action at Bakke Forum," *The Harvard Crimson*, Dec. 15, 1977, https://www.thecrimson.com/article/1977/12/15/ professors-administrators-debate-affirmative-action-at/.

176 "People kept accusing me of not being smart enough": Biskupic, *Breaking In*, 9.

177 Thurgood Marshall's confirmation hearing: Laura Kalman, *The Long Reach of the Sixties: LBJ, Nixon, and the Making of the Contemporary Supreme Court* (New York: Oxford University Press, 2017), 35, 105.

177 "relatively small capacity for verbal analysis": G. Edward White, *Earl Warren: A Public Life* (New York: Oxford University Press, 1982), 180.

177 "It's the American flag": Ed Cray, *Chief Justice: A Biography of Earl Warren* (New York: Simon & Schuster, 1997), 492.

177 The 1968 case *Levy v. Louisiana*: *Levy v. Louisiana*, 391 U.S. 68 (1968).

178 *New York Times v. Sullivan*: Anthony Lewis, *Make No Law: The Sullivan Case and the First Amendment* (New York: Random House, 1991).

178 Clearance rates on violent crimes: Paul G. Cassell and Richard Fowles, "Handcuffing the Cops? A Thirty-Year Perspective on *Miranda*'s Harmful Effects on Law Enforcement," *Stanford Law Review* 50, no. 4 (April 1998): 1055–145, https://doi.org/10.2307/1229283.

178 small price to pay for enabling the sexual revolution: Bernard Schwartz, *The Unpublished Opinions of the Warren Court* (New York: Oxford University Press, 1985), 227–39.

178 This had the advantage of being nominally consistent: Victoria Smolkin, *A Sacred Space Is Never Empty: A History of Soviet Atheism* (Princeton, N.J.: Princeton University Press, 2018).

179 Released time for religious instruction was okay: Kermit L. Hall, ed., *The Oxford Guide to United States Supreme Court Decisions* (New York: Oxford University Press, 1999).

179 *Schempp* struck down two practices: Leo Pfeffer, *This Honorable Court: A History of the United States Supreme Court* (Boston: Beacon Press, 1965), 422.

180 "Compared to most cud-chewing": Bryan F. Le Beau, *The Atheist: Madalyn Murray O'Hair* (New York: New York University Press, 2003).

181 The black social worker: William K. Muir Jr., *Prayer in the Public Schools: Law and Attitude Change* (Chicago: University of Chicago Press, 1967).

181 Only 5 percent of boomers: Daniel A. Cox, Jacqueline Clemence, and Eleanor O'Neil, *The Decline of Religion in American Family Life: Findings from the November 2019 American Perspectives Survey* (Washington, D.C.: American Enterprise Institute, 2019).

182 In 2016, law schools became more than 50 percent female: Mike Stetz, "Girls Rule: A Number of Law Schools See Female Enrollment Growth," *National Jurist*, Oct. 8, 2019, https://www.nationaljurist.com/national-jurist -magazine/girls-rule-number-law-schools-see-female-enrollment-growth.

182 rates of up to 75 percent: Bureau of Labor Statistics, The Economics Daily, *39 Percent of Managers in 2015 Were Women*, Aug. 1, 2016, https://www.bls .gov/opub/ted/2016/39-percent-of-managers-in-2015-were-women.htm.

183 *Department of Commerce v. New York*: Richard Wolf, " 'The People's Justice': After Decade on Supreme Court, Sonia Sotomayor Is Most Outspoken on Bench and Off," *USA Today*, Aug. 8, 2019, https://www.usatoday.com/ story/news/politics/2019/08/08/justice-sonia-sotomayor-supreme-court -liberal-hispanic-decade-bench/1882245001/.

183 **In 2013 she was so quick:** Josh Blackman, "Transcript Updated: Justice Thomas Said, 'Well, There—See, He Did Not Provide Good Counsel,'" *Josh Blackman's Blog*, Jan. 23, 2013, http://joshblackman.com/blog/2013/01/23/transcript-updated-justice-thomas-said-well-there-see-he-did-not-provide-good-counsel/.

183 **"I cannot tell you":** Joan Biskupic, speech at University of California, Irvine Law School, Sept. 14, 2016, https://www.law.uci.edu/podcast/episode18.html.

183 **He would have preferred:** Bernard Schwartz, *A History of the Supreme Court* (New York: Oxford University Press, 1993), 15.

184 **When Sotomayor crassly asked:** David G. Savage and Michael A. Memoli, "Sotomayor Scheduling Conflict Leads to Biden's Early Swearing In," *Los Angeles Times*, Jan. 18, 2013, https://www.latimes.com/politics/la-xpm-2013-jan-18-la-pn-sotomayor-biden-inauguration-20130118-story.html.

185 **used to strike down changes:** William D. Araiza, *Animus: A Short Introduction to Bias in the Law* (New York: New York University Press, 2017).

186 **"Parliament can do anything except":** Bernard Schwartz, *The Roots of Freedom: A Constitutional History of England* (New York: Hill & Wang, 1967), 97.

187 **forced Summers to publish:** Scott Jaschik, "What Larry Summers Said," *Inside Higher Ed*, Feb. 18, 2005, https://www.insidehighered.com/news/2005/02/18/what-larry-summers-said.

188 **The Faculty of Arts and Sciences:** Alan Finder, Patrick D. Healy, and Kate Zernike, "President of Harvard Resigns, Ending Stormy 5-Year Tenure," *The New York Times*, Feb. 22, 2006, https://www.nytimes.com/2006/02/22/education/22harvard.html.

188 **Socially conservative boilerplate:** David Bernstein, *You Can't Say That: The Growing Threat to Civil Liberties from Anti-discrimination Law* (Washington, D.C.: Cato Institute, 2003), 54–55.

189 **It "can lead to patterns":** Suzanne Lucas, "'OK, Boomer' in the Workplace Can Get You Fired," *Inc.*, Nov. 11, 2019, https://www.inc.com/suzanne-lucas/okay-boomer-in-workplace-can-get-you-fired.html.

CHAPTER 8: THE MILLENNIALS

192 the protests had no effect: Adam Garfinkle, *Telltale Hearts: The Origins and Impact of the Vietnam Antiwar Movement* (New York: St. Martin's Griffin, 1997), chap. 1.

193 The beginnings of guerrilla warfare: Steven M. Gillon, *Separate and Unequal: The Kerner Commission and the Unraveling of American Liberalism* (New York: Basic Books, 2018), 162.

194 Simone de Beauvoir "might have finished her life": Richard Vinen, *A History in Fragments: Europe in the Twentieth Century* (New York: Da Capo, 2001), 113.

194 only 10 percent of whites: Gillon, *Separate and Unequal*, 278.

194 the Black Lives Matter movement: Zack Budryk, "Poll Finds Majority Support for Black Lives Matter, but Opposition to Defunding Police, Reparations," *The Hill*, July 21, 2020, https://thehill.com/policy/508254-americans -largely-support-black-lives-matters-but-dont-back-removal-of-monuments -poll.

196 "a new period of barbarism": Andrew Ferguson, "The End of 'Civilisation,'" *The Weekly Standard*, April 13, 2018, https://www.washington examiner.com/weekly-standard/the-end-of-civilisation.

197 "it was institutions which made society work": Kenneth Clark, "The Quest for Civilization," *The New York Times*, Oct. 7, 1970, https://www.ny times.com/1970/10/07/archives/the-quest-for-civilization-in-art-as-in-life -creativity-cannot-be.html.

Index

INDEX